the innate characters of these individuals that accounts for their achievements. It's the lessons they learned in the Corps— not only about the military life, but about life in general—that have expanded and channeled their abilities. This eminently useful and readable book tells how and why the Marine Corps way works—for a lifetime."

—Walter Anderson, Editor of *Parade Magazine*

Semper Fi

Business Leadership the Marine Corps Way

Dan Carrison
Rod Walsh

AMACOM

American Management Association

New York • Atlanta • Boston • Chicago • Kansas City • San Francisco • Washington, D.C.
Brussels • Mexico City • Tokyo • Toronto

This publication is designed to provide accurate and authoritative
information in regard to the subject matter covered. It is sold with
the understanding that the publisher is not engaged in rendering
legal, accounting, or other professional service. If legal advice or
other expert assistance is required, the services of a competent professional person should be sought.

Library of Congress Cataloging-in-Publication Data

Carrison, Dan.
    Semper Fi : business leadership the Marine Corps way / Dan
Carrison, Rod Walsh.
        p.   cm.
    Includes index.
    ISBN 0-8144-0413-8
    1. Leadership.   2. Employees—Recruiting.   3. Success in business.
I. Walsh, Rod.   II. Title.
    HD57.7.C368   1998
    658.4'092—dc21   98-28370
                                                                 CIP

Printing number

10   9

To my dad, Captain Daniel Carrison, USN, who was a great admirer of the Marines. To my mother, Aurelia. And to my lovely wife, Loan, and my son, James.

To my mother, Evelyn, and my brother, Thomas, who steered me clear of life's early shoals. And, to my beautiful wife, Linda, whose unending patience allowed the completion of this book, and to my kids, Steven, David, and Lou-Enne.

And to the dedicated men and women of the United States Marine Corps, yesterday, today, and forever.

The authors are donating a portion of their royalties on sales of this book to the Marine Corps Toys for Tots program.

In Loving Memory—
To Al Saunders, for his advice and for his friendship.

Contents

Foreword

As a businessman, and a former Marine, I have spent many more years in a pin-striped suit than in a Marine uniform. Yet I have found that the incomparable leadership training I received in the Marine Corps has served me well over the years in the business world.

Marine Corps training prepared me to lead Marines into combat, but many of the lessons I learned are equally applicable to the "battlefield" of the marketplace. The intensely competitive environment of the world of commerce calls for courage, resourcefulness, flexibility, and, above all, the ability to inspire your people to follow you—even when you may be going on instinct alone.

If there was ever an organization with an abundance of *leaders*, at every level of the chain of command, it is the Marine Corps. If the Marine Corps were to be magically transformed into a business overnight, those of us in private enterprise would immediately be aware of the "new kid on the block." The dedication to mission—and the ability of its leaders to inspire those under their authority—would make the Marine Corps in the business world exactly what it is in the military world: a success out of all proportion to its size.

This book is for the business leader, wherever he or she stands on the organizational ladder. Each unique Marine Corps leadership principle is revealed and briefly explained by the authors, and then applied to the competitive world of business. I am confident that the reader will find this book to be a hip pocket reference for leadership—one that he or she will return to time and again.

> Vernon R. Loucks, Jr.
> Chairman and Chief Executive Officer
> Baxter International, Inc.
> Formerly 1st Lieutenant, USMC

Acknowledgments

First, we thank our editor, Ms. Adrienne Hickey, who encouraged and counseled us from start to finish. Without Adrienne we would have been lost at sea. Lt. Colonel Scott Campbell USMC, opened the doors to every Marine base we needed to visit and was always just a phone call away. To Ms. Betty Kilbride, our resourceful research assistant. And to 1st Lieutenant Celeste Ross USMC, our first on-base contact, whose assistance proved to be invaluable.

We benefited from the advice and selfless contribution of time and resources from countless people, including Ms. Betty Adkins, Major Rod Albright, Major Betsy Arends, Gunnery Sergeant Cynthia Atwood, Major Eileen Banks, [Colonel] Barney Barnum, Jr., Medal of Honor recipient—Vietnam, [Colonel] Cary Baumgartner, Lt. Colonel Jeffery Bearor, 1st Lieutenant Ted Benjamin, Captain Warren Blackmon, 1st Lieutenant Renee Bonafe, Dr. James Boulgarides, Master Gunnery Sergeant Andy Brown, Sergeant Major Charles L. Brown III, Major Paula Buckley, Mr. Tom Burke, Staff Sergeant Randy Burns, [Major] Michael P. Capriano, Ms. Brenda Carter, Ms. Lisa Chastain, Colonel Stephen A. Cheney, Major Larry Clayton, Dr. William Cohen, Captain Douglas L. Constant, [Lt. General] Matthew Cooper, [Sergeant] Nicholas Corea, Gunnery Sergeant Carlos M. Craig, Ms. Becky Crokett, Captain Scott Cubbler, Colonel Richard J. Dallaire, Mr. William A. Davey,

Note: Those whose ranks are bracketed are either in the USMC Reserve or are former Marines.

1st Lieutenant Liz Donnell, [Lt. Colonel] Jeff Dorroh, Lt. Colonel Frank Duggan, Captain Charles Egerton, Ms. Leilani Eleccion, [Major] John Elliott Jr., Mrs. Chris Ewalt, Mrs. Kelly Farmer, Mr. Haisam M. Farran, Mr. John P. Fitzgerald, Sergeant Major Jimmy Forest, Staff Sergeant Doug Fraser, Captain Jesse Garcia, 1st Lieutenant Wendy Garrity, [Corporal] Michael J. Gehrig, Ms. Pam Gildersleeve, Gunnery Sergeant Gregory Gillispie, 1st Lieutenant Cliff Gilmore, Reverend Monsignor John J. Graham, Mr. Pete Haas, Lt. Colonel Ellen Katie Haddock, [Captain] Doug Hamlin, [Master Sergeant] Charles P. Handschuh, [Colonel] Kevin P. Hart, First Sergeant Richard A. Hawkins, [Lt. Colonel] Hamilton E. Hicks Jr., Lt. Colonel Ernest Hickson, Sergeant Major Stanley C. Hillery, Lt. Colonel Jenny Holbert, Staff Sergeant Glenn Holloway, Captain Jeffrey C. Holt, [Colonel] James A. Homan, 1st Lieutenant Zack Jacobson, Gunnery Sergeant Helen A. Josypenko, 1st Lieutenant Themie Karavites, Mr. Johnny Keene, Miss Linda Kiernan, Master Sergeant Rick Kinietz, the Konjoyan Family, Major Nancy LaLuntas, Staff Sergeant John LaMantia, [Captain] Joseph Larkin, Colonel Robert E. Lee, Lt. Colonel William Leek, [Colonel] David J. Leighton, [Colonel] Jim Leslie, Captain John Lincoln, [Brigidier General] Fred Lopez, [1st Lieutenant] Vernon R. Loucks Jr., Staff Sergeant Rodney W. Lowe, Sergeant Chad McBeen, Major Carol McBride, [Lt. Colonel] Peter McCarthy, [Captain] David McClary, Major Rob McClary, Captain Krista A. McKinley, [Corporal] John A. (Jack) McLean, Lance Corporal Sharon Metivier, [Major] Tony Meyers, [Lt. Colonel] J. Todd Miles, Sergeant Mandi A. Miller, Captain John C. Milliman, [Lt. Colonel] Edmund C. Mitchell, Sergeant Gary Mokuau, 1st Lieutenant Wendy Moratta, PFC Nalley, Staff Sergeant Claudia Nelson, [Lt. Colonel] George G. Ogilvie, Staff Sergeant Jose Padilla, [Corporal] Tony Palminteri, 1st Lieutenant Melanie Papatestas, Brigadier General Garry Parks, Mrs. Anja Partin, Lance Corporal Gregory Pentacost, Sergeant Major Ray Phillips, Sergeant Major Lou Porras, [Sergeant] Jay Proctor, Mr. Arnie Regardie, Staff Sergeant Arthur Rodriguez, 1st Lieutenant John Ross, 1st Lieutenant Jeff Sammons, Captain

Steve Sklenka, Ms. Allison Smith, [Captain] Frederick W. Smith, Major George W. Smith Jr., Captain Dave Steele, [Captain] James H. Stone, [Major] Charles A. Sullivan, [Captain] Arthur Ochs Sulzberger Sr., [Colonel] William F. Sutherland, [Sergeant] Eric Svenonius, Gunnery Sergeant Bryan Swanson, [Staff Sergeant] Tyrone Talbert, Sergeant Tracy Tanna, [Lance Corporal] Najmah Tappin, Ms. BettyAnn Thompson, Sergeant Mauricio Torres, [Lt. Colonel USAF] Ronald L. Tottingham, Captain Michelle L. Trusso, Captain Kristi L. Van Gorder, Lance Corporal David Vatungbapal, Staff Sergeant Porfirio Velasquez, Lt. Commander (USN) J. Barry Walsh, Gunnery Sergeant Paul Washington, Gunnery Sergeant Sophia Webb, [Major] Will Weisenburg, [Master Sergeant] Mike West, Sergeant Major William I. Whaley, [Lt. Colonel] Arthur E. White, Gunnery Sergeant Gary Wilder, [Captain] Millie Wilkerson, Major Greg Wilson, Captain Steve Wolf.

Introduction

The business community is justifiably fascinated by the concept of leadership. Corporations and small businesses collectively spend millions of dollars annually on programs to educate, inspire, and motivate their personnel toward achieving the ambitious goals possible in today's marketplace. All too often, however, the search for effective leadership principles is frenetic. Companies hail one method as the definitive path into the future, only to throw the baby out with the bathwater three years later in favor of some new and improved concept. Thinking "out of the box" is applauded, while classic business case studies are dismissed as fairy tales of the pre-Internet age. Technology is worshipped; seminar gurus prepare us for the twenty-first century as if it will be the dawn of an entirely new, cybernetic human nature. Young and aggressive CEOs are demanding "state-of-the-art" business strategies and the leaders to implement them, suitable for the brave new world awaiting us all.

Ironically, in the search for leadership principles, businessmen and women often overlook that which makes their pursuit even possible. Were it not for the highly successful leadership principles practiced by the United States military, the world as we know it would be a vastly different place. Our very way of life depends upon the ability of our military leaders to inspire and direct personnel at all levels, often under unimaginable stress. The military has long understood the critical need for leadership throughout the ranks, the cost of failure being so catastrophic. There is no such thing as Chapter 11 protection from the enemy on the eve of defeat.

If Harvard Business School were to include, and then prioritize, major military events in their famous Case Studies curriculum, there would be little class time left for even the most well-known industrial and commercial sagas. The largest corporate mergers would be dwarfed by the vast military alliances of World War II; the logistical feats of the greatest industrialists would seem insignificant next to the colossal accumulation of men and material assembled for D day (which was all the more amazing because it was planned and carried out in complete secrecy); and the most inspiring corporate "comeback" would appear mundane next to the story of America's struggle for survival during the dark years that followed the crippling attack on Pearl Harbor.

The American public had an opportunity to witness the efficiency of the nation's armed forces more recently, during Desert Storm. Perhaps even more impressive than the swift military victory against Iraq was the logistical miracle that made it possible. In the middle of the desert, a virtual city was erected, with facilities to support nearly one million men and women—not to mention an overwhelming tank invasion into fortified Iraq—and more than two thousand aircraft landings and takeoffs a day (more than the nation's busiest airports). Instead of having years to accomplish this impossible task, our generals had three months.

While all branches of the American armed forces produce effective leaders, there is one service that stands alone. The United States Marine Corps—the smallest service with the biggest reputation—has been refining its own unique methods of leadership cultivation for more than two hundred years. Marine Corps training is different from that of the army, navy, and air force, and the men and women who emerge from it are different. And, while every branch of the armed forces has elite units, the Marine Corps as an entity is elite, and those who choose to join know full well an easier road could have been taken.

The authors, both former Marines and now successful businessmen, are convinced that managers at all levels have a lot to learn from today's Marine Corps, when it comes to instilling leadership throughout the ranks of an organization. Contrary to the Hollywood conception, Marine Corps leadership is not a matter of barking sergeants and intimidated troops. Men and women Marines *want* to go the extra mile; they have been inspired by their training and by the culture created within "the Corps" to a degree not easily understood by those on the outside, but that is certainly attainable in other settings as well. Their motto, Semper Fidelis—which means Always Faithful—is more than a catchy phrase to those who have served; they are words to live by.

Semper Fi: Business Leadership the Marine Corps Way presents the unique leadership principles that have been developed by the Marine Corps over time, as well as the bold, groundbreaking training innovations coming out of the Marine Corps today, and shows how they can be, and have been, applied with great success to the workplace. *Semper Fi* begins with the successful recruiting techniques of the Marine Corps and demonstrates how the business community would do well to emulate them, if it wishes to attract and retain the best applicants possible. The authors examine the leadership cultivation techniques employed in boot camp, Sergeant's School, Officer's Training, all the way up the chain of command to the General Staff. At each step, they show how today's managers, at equivalent levels, can and should implement these principles within their own organizations. Finally, Marine Corps strategies for victory—the end result of successful leadership—are shown to be just as applicable to the competitive marketplace as they are to the battlefield.

The results of poor leadership skills in the corporate world, while not as historically dramatic as those on the battlefield, are no less consequential to the fate of a corporation. The degree to which every business prepares its managers to inspire and direct the personnel under their authority will determine its success. When it comes to building leaders, no-body does it better than the United States Marines. The men and women who apply to their own business careers the prin-ciples presented in the pages that follow can become the lead-ers of their generation.

1

Attracting the Best

"We recruit what we are."

—Major General Jack Klimp, head of Marine Corps
Recruiting Command, Washington, DC

"If we want to be the best company for our customers and investors, we must first be the best company for our employees."

—Vernon R. Loucks Jr., Chairman and Chief
Executive Officer, Baxter International Inc.,
formerly 1st Lieutenant, USMC

Organizations are a lot like individuals: They long to be immortal. What is impossible to us singly is somewhat more possible to the organization, if it is able to attract new, qualified men and women, on a timely and recurrent basis, into its ranks. Corporations invest heavily in their own human resources departments—and are willing to simultaneously pay large sums to third-party headhunter agencies—to identify and screen likely candidates. Advertising firms are put on annual retainers to steer the bright and ambitious toward one company, rather than another. Companies preen and strut before the nation's youth at college campuses and job fairs.

But for all the huge expenditure of effort, private enterprise does not hold a candle to the Marine Corps' ability to attract the kinds of people it wants. The Marine Corps "wrote the book" on how to recruit individuals who will be a credit to the organization. Fortunately, these unique techniques are quite adaptable to the recruiting efforts of businesses large and small.

Recruiters Should Be the Cream of the Crop

Any study of Marine Corps recruiting techniques must begin with the recruiter himself (and, in many cases, herself).[1] No amount of funding, marketing, and advertising support can make up for weaknesses in the person behind the desk.

When a young person sits across the desk of a Marine Corps recruiting officer, there is little doubt in the recruit's mind that the person opposite is the real thing. Lean, immaculate in his uniform, a Marine Corps recruiter looks as if he could put down his pen at a moment's notice, grab a machine gun, and lead a squad to glory. Few men are more downright confidence inspiring. Young candidates want to be like him, and they envision Marine Corps training as a transformation. Along with the drill instructor, the recruiter symbolizes in body, appearance, and manner The Few, The Proud, The Marines.

Ironically, nobody joins the Marines to become a recruiter. Young men and women sign up to participate in a vigorous way of life—usually in the infantry—not to sit behind a desk. Action-oriented people generally shy away from duties where communication skills are required; they would rather do something than talk about it. But the best of these rough and ready Marines are selected to complete an extensive course in public speaking and professional selling and training skills. Many balk at the new training requirements, but all will, at

[1] Although every leadership principle highlighted in this book applies to women Marines (as well as to their counterparts in private enterprise), the authors will use, for the sake of convenience, the masculine pronoun throughout the text.

some point in their careers, consider themselves fortunate to be assigned a tour of recruiting duty.

Because attracting the right kinds of individuals is considered so critical for the well-being of the Corps, the recruiting billet is a very high-profile post. Success as a recruiter is a virtual guarantee of promotion; failure, while not career ending, is definitely a negative. So young people who joined the Marines to fight America's battles find themselves not only putting up with professional selling skills classes and Toastmasters clubs but trying to excel. The end product is a persuasive, smooth-talking fighter who can't wait to get back into the field.

Perhaps it is this very eagerness to return to the front that makes the recruiter so credible. A young candidate can sense that the recruiter is a man of action, and the candidate wants to take part also. In a metaphorical sense, Marine Corps recruiters are the kingdom's best knights, sent back from the battlefield into the villages to gather volunteers.

How many companies can say they have sent their "best knights" out onto the college campuses and job fairs to represent them? More often than not, management hires out this critical responsibility to a third party. Headhunters represent the company, taking on the perceived burden of interviewing and screening so many candidates. The very people who should be there, the top managers and salespeople, who are more qualified than anybody else to recognize potential, remain on the front line. Often, companies have no idea of who sits behind the booth with their logo on it.

It is true that many businesses have invested in a human resources department, with employee recruiting as part of its mandate. But the motives are usually of a defensive nature; HR is more often used as a shield against litigation from disgruntled employees than as an aggressive outreach agency for quality recruits. In too many cases, the human resources department "subs out" its recruiting responsibilities to headhunters, abdicating its greatest responsibility.

Do Your "Recruiters" Believe What They Say?

In every sales situation, whether it involves a customer's money or his heart, belief in the product may be the single most compelling factor in that exchange of trust we call a sale. If the company rep does not believe in his product, it will soon become apparent to the customer in front of him. On the other hand, when the belief is a passionate conviction, it is positively contagious.

There is no doubt in the mind of a person considering joining the Marine Corps that the recruiter honestly believes that he belongs to the most elite organization of warriors on the face of the earth. The applicant may well decide that the Marines are not for him, but there will be no question as to the recruiter's conviction. The Marine recruiter will literally lay down his life for the Corps and probably has at one time or another during his career been called to put that life on the line.

Although such complete and total commitment may not be expected in private enterprise, some executive search firms, or headhunters, fall so below the minimum expectations that corporations are often appalled at their lack of loyalty. While there certainly are reputable search firms, many exhibit the faithfulness of a hungry alley cat. The headhunter, generally paid by commission only, must place his applicant somewhere, and soon. He is motivated by a successful placement, rather than by a successful matching of individual talent to companies. A tickler file sits on his desk, alerting him of previously placed applicants who have spent the required one year with the employers he has represented. Soon, it is time for the "Are you still happy there?" phone call. If his old placement is not positively ecstatic, he is informed of an opportunity at XYZ Company.

Is it possible to even imagine a Marine Corps recruiter calling the personnel he placed after their four-year enlistment period to see if they want to join the army? Is it even conceivable that the Marine Corps would delegate one of its most critical functions—recruiting men and women of good character—to outside headhunters?

Many companies, disappointed with third-party search firms, now rely upon their own, in-house human resources departments to recruit new personnel. But many HR people are hired from outside the company—often from the headhunter firms themselves—and have not directly experienced company life long enough, or broadly enough, to become "believers." The Marine Corps would never consider hiring its recruiters from the outside, dressing them in a Marine uniform, and then expect them to exhibit the passionate conviction that should characterize a recruiter.

A company that wishes to develop a recruiting effort that will attract the future leaders of the organization should go about it the Marine Corps way. First of all, HR recruiters should be appointed from within. If you have to hire the litigation specialists from the outside, so be it; but don't let them recruit. Since HR will be a prestigious tour of duty, only the best managers and employees will be assigned. This cream of the crop will serve for only one or two years and will be held to a high performance standard. At the end of their stint, they will be rewarded for a successful tour by promotion to other responsibilities within the company. Other "believers" will follow in their footsteps, delighted to have such a high-profile and important post and to have the opportunity to bring the best people they can find into the organization they love.

Recruiting the Marine Corps Way

Cast a Wider Net

Although the Marine Corps insists upon a number of qualifications for new hires, such as a high school diploma, an absence of a police record, a negative drug test, a sufficient score on the aptitude test, and excellent health, it nonetheless casts a fairly wide net in its recruiting efforts. Many, many different kinds of people are accepted. The recruiting process is not, essentially, a screening-out process. It is an effort to go out into the community and bring in lots of young people of good character—to the tune of 40,000 every year.

Recruiters may have a hunch about who will be natural leaders in boot camp, but they do not exclude applicants who might seem hopelessly deficient in leadership characteristics. On the contrary, a huge number of young people join the Corps precisely because they lack the very qualities Marines exude; they join in the hope of transformation.

The recruiter is confident that the transformation will take place. He can cast a wide net because of his faith in the best training in the world. He knows that most of these young people, from disparate backgrounds, will be forged into a fighting force that will not quit.

It's the training, not the screening, that can put a high school graduate, who may have never driven a car, at the wheel of a fifty-million-dollar tank. The technology may be rocket science, but the recruiter knows that the candidate in front of him doesn't have to be a rocket scientist to drive that tank around. All that is required is "tank school" and the desire to apply oneself.

It's the training, not the screening, that creates Marine Corps leaders of all ranks. Every drill instructor knows that leadership is something to be cultivated and that virtually every recruit has the potential. And every drill instructor has experienced the pleasant surprise of seeing a leader emerge from within the most unlikely of candidates. In fact, those recruits identified early in boot camp as leaders—the ones who take to screaming orders like ducks to water—often do not have the enduring leadership qualities found in their quieter counterparts.

Private enterprise, having neither the confidence nor the patience of the Marine Corps—not to mention the recruiting budget—attempts to begin with the best, through a vigorous screening process. An increasing number of standards must be met—college degree, excellent grade-point average, three years' "related experience," computer expertise in specific software applications—in order to weed out all but the most qualified applicants and in order to reduce the training required. It's the screening, not the training, that management hopes will identify its leaders.

But occasionally corporate management is disappointed in its leaders and wonders why its "whiz kids" haven't delivered. Since only the cream of the crop of applicants survived the weeding-out process, they wonder what went wrong.

By emphasizing its screening procedures, instead of its training, management rarely experiences that pleasant surprise of watching a leader emerge from an unlikely recruit. By focusing on a candidate's accomplishments, instead of relying on the best training in the world to bring out each recruit's potential, companies turn away many future corporate leaders.

Are we suggesting that businesses lower their hiring standards?

In a way, yes.

Rather than make applicants leap over an increasingly raised bar, businesses should instead look for the kinds of qualities the Marines search out and let their training programs do the rest. Qualities such as honesty, determination, and a cheerful acceptance of stress, which can all be identified through probing questionnaires and interviews, may be more important to the company in the long run than one's college grade-point average or years of "related experience." A proper training and management culture will cultivate the leadership qualities desired.

We are not suggesting that past accomplishments should be ignored. The more senior the position being applied for, the more important the credentials on the resume. It must be remembered, however, that *everything* looks good on a resume and that previous experience is difficult to verify and to quantify. Often the interviewer, like the Marine recruiter, must factor in his own impressions of the candidate sitting across from him.

Extol the Appeal of Self-Sacrifice

Army and navy recruiting commercials reach out to Generation X with promises of what the services will give in return for joining: $40,000 toward a college education and a chance to be trained in skills that will be sought after by employers upon the return to civilian life. In contrast, Marine Corps recruiting commercials are distinctive for how little in the way of material benefits are promised.

A typical Marine Corps commercial or advertisement in fact promises nothing. It only asks the question "Do you have what it takes to be one of us?" Implicit in the question, and in the image of the young, squared-away person wearing the Marine Corps uniform, is the promise of transformation into somebody who *does* belong to this elite branch of the service. There is no mention of the Marine Corps' considerable financial contribution to college or of the high-tech skills one will learn and take back into the job market. These are benefits that one derives from belonging to the Marine Corps, certainly, but they're not good reasons to join.

The Marine Corps is not looking for individuals who can be motivated only by material gain. It appeals instead to the smaller number of people who can be inspired by patriotism and by the challenge to see if they've got what it takes to become "one of us." In today's culture, which glorifies instant gratification, this appeal to action without material reward is strangely compelling.

Of course, in private enterprise money is by far the reason most of us choose one company over another. Salary is weighed, along with long-term benefits such as a company car, health coverage, and 401-K savings plan, and the company with the best package generally gets the candidate. Even if we are momentarily tempted to join a firm that offers less money but more interesting work, our spouses, friends, and parents may prevail upon us to remember our responsibilities and to make the practical choice. Money usually wins, and the giant corporations, like the owners of athletic teams, keep raising the ante for America's college talent, so the packages become more and more enticing.

Can a corporation make an appeal to self-sacrifice without being laughed out of existence by the whiz kids in today's job market? It is certainly possible, but only if the corporation has the kind of mystique that can demand sacrifice.

If all employees in a company, from the CEO to the line assembler, believe that they work for the best company in the industry, that they are without peer, and that those who work for the competition do so because they are not qualified to belong to the best in the business, then an applicant may be motivated to join by reasons other than money. If, in the public's imagination, a corporation has the best workers in the industry—as opposed to being the best place to work—then it will attract a certain kind of individual. If the company has a reputation for offering the most complete, albeit rigorous, training in the world, one will feel cheated by working anywhere else.

A corporation cannot develop and sustain this kind of attitude purely through PR. It *really* must offer the best products and services in the business. It really must offer the best training in the marketplace, as well as opportunities for interesting and challenging work. Having done so, it must keep the sense of elitism alive throughout the rank and file—publicly, shamelessly, and constantly—so that all employees feel privileged to be a part of the organization.

Start a Pool Program

One of the reasons for the success of the Marine Corps' recruiting effort is the "pool" program. Instituted in 1995, the pool program is one of the ways recruiters can lessen the psychological and physical shock of arguably the most difficult basic training in the world.

The "poolee," a recruit on a delayed-entry program, is

shown candid videos of boot camp. Although it is one thing to see a film of a drill instructor screaming into another person's ear, and quite another to feel the blast oneself, the video gives the applicant an idea of what is to come. Poolees spend weekend hours learning the fundamentals of drill and the protocol they will be expected to follow. They even learn the words to the Marine Corps Hymn. In every way, they are better prepared for boot camp than the recruit without the benefit of this "heads-up." The results have validated the program, reducing the attrition rate significantly.

There are several ways in which a business can implement a pool program of its own. Companies can introduce themselves to the prospective employee base of the community by well-advertised open houses and factory tours. A "part time only" group could be established so that the company can put on retainer, so to speak, a pool of prospective full-time employees who are already familiar with the corporate culture. An even more forward-looking plan could be arranged with the local high schools and colleges. "Work experience" programs, offering local students a sampling of meaningful employment, would be an excellent PR gesture, as well as a practical way of introducing prospective talent into the organization. Local college students would be delighted to augment their business term papers with actual "office time." Academic credits could be set up, encouraging students to participate in actual business projects—a win-win situation if there ever was one.

Businesses can also participate in government training programs, accepting former welfare recipients as job trainees. Under these circumstances, the government might even pay the trainees' wages, or a share of them. Those who do well in the training will be excellent employee prospects, familiar with the company, grateful for the opportunity, and trained essentially "for free."

These kinds of programs require a commitment from the company, which must invest time and energy into the community. Calling a headhunter to fill an immediate vacancy may be easier, but it will never fill up the pipeline with quality candidates. A pool program benefits all. While your prospective employees are looking you over, you're looking them over.

Start a "Buddy System"

One of the most successful Marine Corps recruiting concepts is the buddy system. Two friends who might be otherwise unprepared to readily take on the challenges of boot camp alone can enlist together with the guarantee that both will go through basic training in the same unit, and, assuming both qualify for the identical specialty (e.g., infantry, tanks, artillery), continue throughout their hitch together. The buddy system is very appealing for young people who have been friends through high school and who are eager to begin a big adventure together. The prospect of leaving home to join the rugged Marine Corps isn't quite so daunting with a friend along. It is an especially great inducement to know that one won't be alone, and scared to death, during boot camp. Under the buddy system, they can be scared to death, together.

It is important to note that the Marine Corps considers the buddy system to be inviolate. It is not a gimmick, but a promise that is honored. Drill instructors in basic training know which individuals have enlisted together and allow them to bunk side by side and to do most assignments as a team. Why shouldn't they? The whole purpose of basic training is to create a sense of brotherhood between strangers; those who enter the Corps already as "brothers" have a head start.

There is no reason why a company couldn't make a similar commitment to two friends, just out of school, who are wondering which direction to take. A corporate recruiting booth on a college campus, for example, that offered a "buddy system" might have enormous appeal for two young men or women, who like the idea of beginning a business career with a friend's support. Given that both are equally qualified, the company should welcome the pair; after all, it has just filled two job openings and has gotten the extra benefit of a "built-in" morale mechanism for free.

A corporate buddy system would be especially appropriate, but certainly not limited to, the lower levels of the pay scale, which traditionally have the greatest turnover. In fact, turnover is often such a problem that companies offer referral bonuses to existing employees who can suggest reliable acquaintances to join the workforce. Why not save the bonus and simply hire a pair of applicants who come in as "buddies"? The company would commit to keeping them together during training, work shifts, and assignments. In return, management would increase the chances of retaining the employees, who are both "in the same boat." The manager can also make use of a more natural mentoring process; if one of the pair is not performing up to expectations, the buddy can help the low-performing employee acquire the lacking job skills.

Guarantee Career Paths

Years ago, the promises of an armed forces recruiter were considered slightly less credible than those of a rainmaker. A recruiter's "guarantee" was the stuff of jokes, considered worthless. Many an enlistee felt as if he had been "had"— although, of all the services, the Marine Corps' promises must have been the least disingenuous. Every recruit knew coming in that, as a Marine, he would be the first to fight. That was usually why he picked the Marines in the first place.

Today's Marine Corps actually guarantees, in writing, a candidate's career path. If the young recruit wants to be trained in a specific occupation (although he will be a rifleman first), or join a certain unit, or serve in a foreign country of choice, it can all be arranged before signing on the dotted line. The young man or woman who enters the Marines today does so in the sure and certain knowledge of a guaranteed career path.

Usually, in the business world, the first position along the perceived career path is guaranteed, because individuals apply for a certain job initially and are hired. But, from that moment on, in many companies, all bets are off. The new employee, who envisioned a fast track to higher and more rewarding responsibilities, may languish for years in a slot he considers "entry level." Sometimes, the opposite can occur; he may experience too much movement, to different departments or responsibilities. Salespeople are often frustrated by multiple transfers to different product groups. As soon as a salesperson develops some expertise and a fledgling client base for widgets, upper management orders a move to a different division, to compensate for the turnover there.

Salespeople are often the victims of job interview hyperbole, as well. Many a "rep" has discovered upon reporting for duty, after the obligatory two weeks' notice given to the other company, that the terms that had seemed so clear the day of the interview have now been slightly modified. The sales territory isn't quite as large as originally described. The account list is missing a few of the prestigious companies that had prompted the decision to accept the offer. The quota, the manager explains, has been adjusted slightly upward by the "bean counters at headquarters." There was apparently a misunderstanding about the car allowance. That evening, the new salesperson drives home wondering how to explain to the spouse that new hires at the company aren't vested in the benefits plan for a year.

Of course, the job interview hyperbole flow is not one-directional. Prospective employees may exaggerate their previous performance, understate their own weaknesses, and completely fabricate the reasons for leaving their last job. Managers know full well at the very moment of the "welcome aboard" handshake that, twelve months down the line, there may be another, sadder, "best of luck" handshake. But the manager must do his or her very best to at least live up to the company's part of the bargain.

And, while no organization, including the Marine Corps, can absolutely, unequivocally, guarantee an individual's career path without a crystal ball, certain steps can be taken to ensure that the promises made during the interviewing process will not be forgotten. A proactive HR department—one that acts on behalf of the employee, as well as the company—can go a long way toward ensuring that the newly hired associate will be both a personal and a corporate success. Quarterly reviews, over lunch, without the presence of management, can assess the individual's satisfaction with the pace of his development. Goals can be set, and the progress toward them evaluated at the next quarterly meeting. The employee can commit to action plans, such as taking more training classes. In return, HR can promise to represent the earnest efforts of the employee to management.

Make Use of Annual Contracts and Bonuses

Due to the contractual nature of the enlistment period, the military in general knows when one of its own will be tempted to return to civilian life. In other branches of the service, the "short-timer" is contacted by a solicitous reenlistment specialist only months before the enlistment period ends. In the Marines, where there is an ongoing effort to retain existing personnel, the courting begins long before the contracts begin to expire. A Marine who is on track for promotion, who is taking continued educational courses, and whose future tours of duty have been guaranteed is much less likely to return to civilian life. But, even if the Marine is tempted, one of the most compelling arguments for remaining in the Corps for another four years is the comparatively sizable bonus that is offered. Many a Marine has handed over a fifteen-thousand-dollar bonus check to a spouse to soften the news of reenlistment.

Business, although quick to remind its employees that they are replaceable, does not like turnover. The cost of rehiring and retraining, not to mention the associated downtime and lost revenue, behooves management to hang on to its personnel. Certainly one of the most unpleasant surprises a manager can experience is the abrupt resignation of a valued employee. It is at this point (and, regrettably, often only at this point) that management earnestly tries to communicate with the individual, who may have been dissatisfied for years. The company's sudden concern is too little, too late.

Annual employment contracts have a way of keeping both management and the rank and file on their toes. The employee is motivated to perform so that the agreement is renewed, and management is reminded of the value of its associate, who is about to become a free agent. There is also a measure of security for both levels. Management can count on an associate's participation for the year, and the employee will not experience the anxiety of a day-to-day relationship that might leave him open to other offers. Annual agreements also make it possible for both parties to part civilly if the relationship is just not working out. But, rather than coming as a surprise, the resignation is expected *to the day,* which gives management ample time to find a replacement.

Corporate "reenlistment" bonuses could also be used as inducements to retain valuable existing personnel. The bonus would be issued anyway, as a holiday, or a performance bonus, or as part of a profit-sharing plan, so why not bundle it into the annual contract? Since most companies have annual employee reviews, the tasks of evaluating an individual's performance over the previous year and signing him up for another year can be accomplished at one meeting. The employee walks away with a tidy bonus, and the manager can count on stability in that company slot for one more year.

Those companies that do not "believe in" employment agreement renewals should examine the many annual contracts they already make use of without batting an eye. Executives sign annual equipment maintenance contracts routinely, as well as cellular phone agreements and automobile leases. They are eager to sign annual purchase commitments in order to lock in pricing and supply and to remove uncertainty in their dealings with vendors and customers. Yet they leave their most valuable asset of all—their employees—anxious and susceptible to rumor.

Institute the "Tour of Duty"

Another concept the company could adopt is the "tour of duty." Not to be confused with the enlistment period of four years, the tour of duty is the Marine's job assignment, usually lasting one to three years; a Marine can have more than one tour of duty during each enlistment period. As each assignment comes to an end, the Marine may opt to remain, especially if the assignment is the American Embassy in Paris. On the other hand, after twelve months at sea, a Marine may apply for a transfer as soon as the ship docks. In each case, the Corps tries to meet the Marine's wishes. Knowing that the Corps takes individual preferences into account, the Marine does not feel trapped in a particular professional position.

Employees, too, could sign on for a year's tour of duty, at a certain department, branch, or product line. Having the option to extend their stay or to apply for a lateral move into another assignment would give most employees a much appreciated sense of autonomy. Tours of duty could also be mandatory. If the company policy is to groom for management by exposure to many different departments and responsibilities, an employee might feel fortunate to be transferred at the end of each year into another slot. Even the unwelcome assignments would be interpreted as an investment in the employee's value to the company.

Routine reassignments are especially appropriate for some highly sensitive departments. Whenever we read of a scandalous embezzlement case, it always seems to be the most trusted, long-term employee who has been exposed. An institutionalized policy of moving associates around every year may not turn a fundamentally dishonest person into an honest one, but it can certainly make such white-collar crimes much more difficult to commit.

Zero Pressure to "Sign Today"

Unlike the popular conception of a military recruiter who virtually shanghais unsuspecting young people into the service with high-pressure sales tactics, the Marine Corps recruiter does not want to push anybody where he does not want to go. The boot camp experience is tough enough to endure even when one is totally prepared for it; a recruit who enters those gates plagued with self-doubt is walking into a nightmare.

"We're in no hurry to sign up a recruit," says Master Gunnery Sergeant Andy Brown, arguably the most successful recruiter in the Marine Corps.

> "We don't want warm bodies; we want commitment. If a guy can't make up his mind, and keep it made up for a few days, or weeks, he's not going to be right for the Marine Corps. We tell our applicants to go home first and talk to their parents, and their girlfriends. We'll be happy to come along to represent the Corps. When that young man signs on the dotted line, everybody should be on board."

A corporation's human resources department is under a similar obligation to find new associates who demonstrate commitment. Whenever an HR representative speaks of "snagging" a prospect, or of "stealing" somebody from another company, he runs a substantial risk of losing his "catch" once the new employee has had time to consider the ramifications of a hurried decision. Another approach, one that uses less overt pressure but a great deal of "wining and dining," has its own traps. HR should never confuse an applicant with events that will never be repeated. Too much attention, while flattering to a prospect, does not prepare him for the day-to-day work ethic he will be expected to follow.

An HR rep should never act out of fear of losing a prospect to another company, or to another headhunter. And he should never allow himself to be "held up" by the applicant's requirements for joining. (Imagine a Marine Corps recruiter's response to a candidate who threatened to join the army or navy unless his demands were met.) The company recruiter must remember that he represents the best organization in the industry and that, if anybody is going to demonstrate commitment, it will be the applicant. We're not suggesting he should be arrogant. Marine Corps recruiters are solicitous, they want the young person sitting on the other side of the desk to join up. But the decision must be freely and confidently made, and only the applicant knows when it is the right thing to do. The training of new personnel, whether they are Marines or corporate "soldiers," simply costs too much to be thrown away on the uncommitted.

Publicize the Pay Scale

Although money is not motivation for joining the Marine Corps (and, if it were, the recruiter would take a long hard look at the candidate sitting across his desk) the recruiter is pleased to share with all the pay scale. Every recruit, and every Marine, can look at the matrix chart of "Time in Grade and Pay" and see what the future holds in terms of income. There are no secrets. Every Marine knows approximately what his associates earn, all the way up to the Commandant himself. There are no rumors that Sergeant Kowolski "cut a good deal" with his boss and is entitled to more vacation than the rest of the base, or that Captain Jones is "pulling down" more than Captain Smith.

In the corporate culture, there are few matters more private than one's personal income. Paychecks, or automatic deposit receipts, are mailed in security envelopes. We tactfully look away when a nearby associate tears open the envelope, and we wouldn't dream of asking anybody, at work or play, their annual income. But we do wonder, sometimes aloud, what our peers and superiors earn. Rumors of huge paychecks inadvertently seen by secretaries abound and, true or false, contribute to a general air of speculation—and sometimes suspicion—that can rapidly demoralize the workplace. Since personal income is a topic that cannot, in good etiquette, be broached, rumors can never be confirmed or denied (few of us would deny, anyway, a rumor that inflated our income).

If one employee were to ask another what he "made for a living," the answer would probably be that it was none of his business. But, is that entirely true? It may be very much his business if the rumor is true that his peer, who has just arrived from another company, is making 25 percent more a year for doing the exact same job. Taking "no comment" as a confirmation of his suspicions, this longtime employee may harbor a resentment against his company that could manifest itself in any number of ways. And, the tragedy is that his resentment may be totally unjustified; in fact, the newcomer may be earning less than his senior and simply be unwilling to admit to it. There is no doubt that management, by protecting the privacy of its employees, had the best of intentions. But a completely unnecessary obstacle to the successful completion of the corporate mission may have been created. A working environment rife with distracting speculation is truly a house divided against itself.

Management might consider publishing the pay scale so that every salaried employee knows where he stands today and what he can strive for in the future. Commissioned employees, as well, would appreciate knowing that there is an objective, standardized base pay schedule, shared by all commissioned associates—or, if not shared, then structured so that all levels are objectively achievable.

There would still be some room for privacy. The matrix does not, for example, have to show one annual dollar figure; it could be a range, separated by thousands of dollars. And there is, of course, the bonus factor, which can't be published because it is after the fact, based on performance at the end of the year. The criterion for bonuses and their formulas would be published—and be objectively achievable for all—but the year-end results would be between the employee and his W-2 statement. A major cause for rampant speculation within the workplace, however, could be removed. Every associate in the company could feel that he was participating in a program that was fair to all, with a potential for increased income that was open to all.

Consolidate Recruiting and Employee Training

As of the late 1970s, the Marine Corps decided to place the responsibilities of recruiting and basic training under one commanding officer, thus breaking a long-held tradition of separating the two functions.

"When you think about it, it makes sense," says Lt. Colonel William Leek, commanding officer of the Los Angeles Recruiting Station. "Recruiting and basic training are two sides of the same coin. Why have two commanders for what is essentially one process, the making of Marines?"

The commanding general in charge of recruiting and basic training is responsible for the end product, the graduate Marine. The Corps feels that the person who has the responsibility must also be given control over the entire process. This way, the commanding officer can't grumble about the quality of recruits being sent into boot camp; he himself brought in the recruits. Conversely, he can't complain that basic training is not bringing out the best in his quality recruits; he is in charge of boot camp. Clearly, the buck stops at his desk. The young Marines replenishing the ranks are a reflection of his ability to command and control the entire process of transformation from civilian into warrior. An added plus is the ability of the commanding officer to hold recruiters responsible for the success of the young men they have brought into the Corps. If a recruiter were ever tempted to sign up a warm body off the street just to meet his quota, he would regret it later, when the young man proved to be a poor investment. The drill instructor, too, is evaluated in part on the number of his recruits who do not make it through boot camp.

Businesses, too, have recruiting and basic training functions, usually under separate managers and separate budgets. The manager in charge of the training process may grumble that he "does his best with the incompetents HR is grabbing off the streets." And the head of HR may dread sending his bright young prospects to the "dullest classes since high school chemistry." Meanwhile, the CEO wonders at the lack of "pizzazz" in the finished product.

Placing both of these critical functions under one head virtually eliminates the potential for friction between otherwise distinct departments. One manager controls one process: the transformation of "civilians" into aggressive and creative corporate "soldiers." There is one budget to deal with, making quick decisions possible, since approval from the other department is no longer necessary. As in the Marine Corps, recruiting and training become sides of the same coin.

Integrating the two functions also gives the newly hired employee confidence in the direction of the organization. There is nothing more disconcerting to the newcomer than to sense friction between those who introduced him into the company and those who took over from there. He feels, instead, that everybody is "on board," with him, and on the way toward a common goal.

Exalt HR

It may come as a surprise to learn that the Marine Corps considers recruiting duty a premier assignment. A successful tour of duty as a recruiter is a virtual guarantee of promotion. But these bright prospects are tempered by the penalty of failure; an unsuccessful tour can mean the end of a Marine's career. When all is said and done, a Marine officer or NCO will look back upon his years in the Corps and either shudder or smile at the memory of recruiting duty. His performance during that one tour of duty may have had the greatest impact, for better or for worse, on his career.

Why would the world's most elite fighting force consider a tour of duty in Human Resources to be just as prestigious as more warlike assignments, such as infantry or tank duty?

The Marine Corps believes that an excellent recruiting program is just as important to the ultimate survival of the Corps as success on the battlefield. The task is daunting: forty thousand men and women of good character must be found, and then brought into the Corps, every single year. But if the wrong kinds of people are accepted out of desperation into only a few recruiting substations, the consequences can be pandemic. Gangs and drug dealers have penetrated every major city in America; each one of these cities has a Marine Corps recruiter guarding the doorway into his beloved Corps.

It is this insistence on "recruiting what we are" that makes the Marines so different from other, even well-known, elite fighting forces. The French Foreign Legion may have a formidable reputation for valor on the battlefield, but it is also famous for its "no questions asked" acceptance policy. In literature, it has consistently been portrayed as a haven for an eclectic assortment of saints and sinners. Service in the Foreign Legion even seems to have taken on a connotation of social redemption, changing the lives of rogues with its rigid discipline. In contrast, the United States Marine Corps is famous for its fighting ability *and* for the stalwart character of those who wear the uniform. Mothers and fathers are proud to say, "My son [or daughter] is a Marine." And this will be true only as long as every recruiter in every city casts a discerning eye on those who walk into his office.

Are poor recruiting practices less consequential to the fate of a corporation? Clearly, every business is only as good as the people it brings into the organization. No function is more important to the ultimate survival of the company than human resources. And yet, how many companies consider HR to be a prestigious "tour of duty," or even a "tour" at all? Most HR personnel stay in HR throughout their time with the company. They are not envied and respected by their fellow employees, nor are they particularly well treated by upper management. HR is basically the hired gun to protect the company against employee litigation. HR personnel are generally brought in from the outside and never really become a part of the company culture. To managers of other departments, HR is not a golden rung on the ladder of success within the organization. It is simply the department they call when they need a witness.

If the world's finest fighting force assigns only its best people to a three-year challenge in recruiting, and then rewards them afterwards with promotion, why shouldn't corporate America make HR a similar rite of passage for its most promising managers?

Make Your HR Office Something Special

As Spartan as a Marine recruiter's office is—and they are indeed Spartan—the room is nonetheless amply supplied with brochures illustrating the numerous opportunities available within the Marine Corps, as well as its glorious history. The recruiter's presentation binder is a thing of beauty and seems to answer every question an applicant might have. The floors gleam; the desks are polished. Everything in the office, including the recruiter himself, reinforces the candidate's decision to join the Marines.

In private enterprise, the human resources office is the prospective employee's first introduction to the corporation. Management must realize that the company is being appraised from the moment a bright, discerning candidate enters through the door. If he is greeted by a cheerful receptionist and led to an office that exhibits signs of good taste and stability, he will be pleasantly biased before the interview even begins.

The HR representative should look every bit the "corporate soldier"—neat, well dressed, the real thing. He should be thoroughly familiar with the company, and its most enthusiastic advocate. Brochures should be presented in a positive manner, perhaps in a way that puts both individuals on the same side of the desk so that pictures and performance graphs can be elaborated upon. If the phone rings, the candidate will be gratified to see that it is instantly forwarded and that no interruptions are being allowed. The HR representative should be excited about the opportunity being discussed and, at the same time, solicitous of the concerns or questions raised by the prospect. At the end of the interview, as the candidate is escorted back to the lobby, he should notice that everyone they meet on the way treats the HR "rep" with courtesy and respect.

If the company has no one office dedicated to human resources, that's fine, as long as a prospective employee is not interviewed in a cubicle, subject to all the noises—and the listening ears—of those in the surrounding cubicles. A clean, conference room is sufficient, enhanced with portable displays of corporate history and opportunity. Every branch office should have the identical PR "kit," like those used at booths on college campuses, to transform a conference room into a window on the corporation. Candidates should be surrounded with images of the company's prestige, and of the career paths available within. As the coffee is poured for him, he should consider himself fortunate to be interviewing with such a class organization.

Ceremonialize Your Employee's First Day

Once an individual has been accepted into the Corps, at an appointed time he or she stands in a room filled with other accepted candidates and awaits the taking of the oath. A solemn officer or NCO in dress blues comes to the front of the room, stands by the American flag, and surveys the young people before him for a grave, silent moment. He raises his own right hand and asks them to raise theirs. With the demeanor of one who is renewing his own pledge, the officer then leads the oath of allegiance. As serious faces look back at him, aware of the solemnity of the moment, the words are repeated with a sincerity that seems to nearly frighten some of the recruits, unaccustomed to making irrevocable commitments. Afterward, amid the handshakes and congratulatory remarks, the sense of awe and irreversibility lingers in each recruit. They have spoken, perhaps for the first time in their young lives, words that cannot be retracted. There is no turning back. They are in the Marine Corps, for real.

The sense of commitment that accompanies a formal oath can certainly be duplicated at a company induction. While incoming employees cannot be required to take an oath, nothing stops the company from formally declaring its commitment to them. The new employees could be shown into a conference room, filled with all the available managers from every department within the organization, as well the people in the departments they will join. The highest-ranking executive in the room could then stand and, in a sincere and friendly manner, pledge the support of the organization to the new associates, expressing the gratitude of the company for being the one chosen by the applicants.

One can imagine the emotional impact of such a scene upon the new employees. As soon as they had the opportunity to say anything, they would no doubt respond in kind, voluntarily pledging their own commitment to the beaming faces of their new associates. Amid the congratulatory handshakes and back slaps, even the most cynical job hopper would be emotionally moved and determined to repay this gesture with earnest effort.

Corporations can also learn from the Marine Corps' experience in helping recruits begin to feel comfortable in their new surrounding—and from the changes the Corps has made in its own procedures. Years ago, a Marine arriving at a new base in the middle of the night would be lucky to find that he was even expected. An indifferent sentry might tell him the location of his new unit, leaving him to find the building, an empty bunk within it, blankets, sheets, and so on. The Marine, accustomed to the "no-frills" way of military life he had volunteered for, may have thought nothing of it. He would be very surprised by the way the "new man" is welcomed in today's Marine Corps.

A modern-day Marine reporting for duty at a new location is welcomed by a base representative—in dress uniform—and two or three members of his new unit, who greet him as if he were a long-awaited reinforcement. He is taken on a tour of the base and acquainted with its amenities. He is shown his room, has dinner with his new buddies, and is made to feel at home. All of this is a conscious effort on the part of the Marine

Corps to make the individual Marine feel that he is an important member of the team, no matter where in the world duty will take him. This kind of overture is contagious, and he treats other Marines—new and old alike—with similar respect.

If only this were typical of the workplace! So often, the newly hired employee must fend for himself, like the Marine of yesteryear. The proper introductions have not been made throughout the department, forcing him to reintroduce himself time and again, lest he be thought of as a customer, or a lost visitor. He must fend for himself, equipping his office or cubicle, and does not know whom to contact regarding payroll deductions, health benefits, and other personnel matters. Not feeling welcomed himself, he may very well treat other incoming employees accordingly.

The corporation that wishes to be revered by its employees must make each one feel special. First impressions endure, even if somewhat unfairly. Fortunately, the company has full control over the employee's first impression. It can make the first day of work a pleasurable affirmation—so that the incoming employee feels as if he or she really did make the right choice.

Let us imagine an employee's (we'll call him Tom) reaction if, as he reports to work on his first day, he is welcomed by a company representative who gives him the grand tour of the facility. He is taken to his department, where his manager personally introduces him to each associate, telling a little of Tom's background and achievements. A company newsletter lies on his desk, with an article about *him* on the front page. A new-employee survival kit chock full of all the relevant company information he will need—plus a few surprises, such as real estate and community services information and discount coupons to a local restaurant, beauty parlor, and family amusement park. He also finds on his desk a videotape with a "welcome aboard" message from the CEO, to be played at home with the family.

Tom has lunch with his new friends and hears all about

the company-sponsored bowling league and softball team. During the afternoon, he is taken around and introduced to all the people of the other departments he will be interacting with. At day's end, his associates drop by to wish him good night. His appointed mentor offers his continued support and perhaps invites him and his family to a barbecue that weekend.

Imagine how buoyant Tom would feel on the way home, how anxious he would be to tell his family that, at long last, he has found a company that just might be "the one." He will never forget the kindness shown to him that day, and he will be eager to repay it and to live up to all the flattering things said about him in the newsletter article. It is interesting to note that this kind of positive experience can be created at no cost to the company itself. All that is required is a thoughtful sensitivity to a person's feeling that first day on the job.

Service After Sales

The most successful Marine Corps recruiters stay in touch with their inductees, long after they finish boot camp. Regular phone calls to the graduate Marine, and to the Marine's family, make for a relationship that extends past signing on the dotted line. The new Marine finds himself visiting his recruiter just to say hello. He sees his own boot camp graduation photo on the wall with all the others who have gone through this station. The recruiter asks if he would like to volunteer a few hours on the weekends, working with the "poolees" on the delayed entry program, and he finds himself saying yes. The recruiter's constancy has come full circle; his inductee is now part of the recruiting station family and is spreading the word to his civilian friends that being a Marine is worth all the hassle.

In your job, when was the last time HR called you on the phone just to see how you were doing? Such overtures are so rare that, if made, most employees would immediately suspect that something bad was about to happen. Do you remember all those questions on your employee application, asking about your hobbies, your interests? Has HR ever once referred to them, ever once asked, "Hey, Bob, how's that car restoration going; do Jimmy and Jennifer help you with it, or are they driving their own cars now?"

The HR person who was so friendly and so helpful during the interviewing process now consciously avoids the new hire, reluctant to confront any misunderstandings of the original bargain. Generally speaking, the only time an employee deals with HR is when there is a problem: Either the employee has a grievance, or his manager needs HR as a witness to document a disciplinary warning. No longer the enthusiastic matchmaker between the applicant and the company, HR is a harbinger of trouble.

Even though HR ultimately represents management—just as the recruiter always represents the Marine Corps—there is much that can be done to continue to serve the incoming employee and, by implication, the company as well. A phone call now and then, and a lunch every six months without the presence of the boss, would mean a lot to the most cynical individual. HR could determine if the newcomer is happy with the pace of his development and if his personal life is, on the balance, a happy one. The career path agreed upon during the interviews could be monitored. The employee could commit to action plans such as outside education, while HR could arrange for more in-house training and internal certification programs. Both the employee and HR would feel a sense of partnership, and the company itself would be the better for it.

Leadership Strategies Checklist

—Rotate the company's top performers through a tour of "recruiting duty."
—Build a human resources department of "believers" from within.
—Emphasize training over screening.

—Make the challenge to belong part of the corporate appeal.
—Fill the workforce pipeline with quality candidates.
—Offer a "buddy system" employment inducement.
—Make use of renewal contracts and bonuses.
—Introduce the "tour of duty" concept.
—Don't be in a rush to "snag" a qualified candidate.
—Publicize the pay scale.
—Place hiring and training responsibilities under one senior manager.
—Make human resources a rite of passage for your managers.
—Provide HR with all the necessary tools to attract the best.
—Make HR an active participant in the employee's career planning.
—After the initial "matchmaking," make sure that HR continues to be solicitous of the employee's well-being.

2

Basic Training

"The more you sweat in peace, the less you bleed in war."

—old Marine adage

"David [Ogilvy] ran our company as if he had grown up in the Marine Corps, and I tried to do so after him. David, more than anyone else in the history of advertising, believed in training. He believed that the more one knew about advertising, the more likely one was to practice it successfully. It made sense then and makes sense now. We had far and away the best training programs in the business—training in every discipline: creative, media, research, and account handling. Everyone in the company was trained, from secretaries to Executive Vice Presidents (like me). All this at a time when there was virtually no advertising education—in colleges, business school, or on the job. I learned more in my first year than in the previous fifteen."

—John Elliot, Jr., Chairman Emeritus of Ogilvy & Mather, formerly Major, USMC

Marine Corps boot camp has a reputation for toughness that may overshadow its real achievement, so pertinent to the world of private enterprise. Every year, forty thousand civilians, from every possible background, stumble through the gates of the Recruit Training Depot, not knowing their left foot from their right, to emerge twelve weeks later as competent professionals, well schooled in the arts of war. Although years of continued training await them, the graduates of boot camp are already the envy of militaries all over the world. Technically proficient, they also embody the esoteric lore of The Corps—its traditions, its spirit, and its nearly obsessive preoccupation with combat readiness. Each recruit has learned the Marine Corps Way, through a superbly engineered curriculum of classroom and field instruction. Each individual represents the whole; and each has become, to some degree, a leader. Every twelve weeks the Marine Corps accomplishes an astonishing indoctrination, which simultaneously conforms the individual and releases him—into an unlimited potential for achievement.

Training is no less critical to the success of a company in private enterprise. Internal procedures and knowledge must be imparted, but so must the corporate philosophy. What fundamentally distinguishes one company from another is the degree to which their future leaders—at every level of responsibility—share the corporate vision. Everything else being equal, the best trained managers and personnel usually win. Most businesses recognize this and have implemented some sort of procedure for the indoctrination of their associates, from impromptu OJT (on-the-job-training) to formal classes taught by professional instructors. But few companies, large or small, are aware of the ease with which many highly successful Marine Corps leadership principles can be applied to their own "basic training."

The Promise of Boot Camp

While all branches of the military have vigorous basic training programs, Marine Corps boot camp is in a category all its own. Its reputation for toughness is so legendary that the army, navy, and air force do not even try to compare their basic training, unless it is to stress that theirs is less strenuous. Marine Corps boot camp is so arduous that it has become the last puberty rite civilization has to offer, in which boys are turned into men. And the horror stories of boot camp only serve to attract those wishing for that kind of transformation all the more.

The promise of Marine Corps boot camp, implicit in all the recruiting advertisements, is transformation: that lean, mean fighting machine on the poster can be you. Moreover, the transformation is permanent, or, in the words of a Marine Corps poster, "The Change Is Forever." This invitation is open to all men and women of good character; all one has to bring is an earnest attitude, and the Marine Corps will supply the rest.

This is really an incredible promise; in fact it is a virtual guarantee, one that attracts all sorts of individuals. The meek yearn to be changed for the better, and the tough want to test their mettle. Even heavyweight boxing champion Riddick Bowe was lured by the promise of boot camp. (Bowe, whose only loss in the ring was to Evander Holyfield, lasted eleven days.)

But the promise of transformation need not be proprietary to the Marine Corps. Businesses can publicly offer a training program so intense, so well conducted, that it will turn the individual into the best at his or her profession whether or not the person stays with the company. The company has to be totally fearless on this point and accept the risk that its "boot camp" will increase the marketability of everyone who is fortunate enough to go through it. In fact, the basic training should be a credential, universally respected. Then, once the company has created the best employees in the industry, it has to do what it takes to keep them.

Some corporate training does have such an aura. IBM is noted for its sales school. Outsourced programs such as the Karris negotiating seminars and Dale Carnegie courses have formidable reputations. But, for the most part, the business community plays it close to the vest. Even well-run company training schools are not publicly touted, perhaps for fear of exposure to the competition, which is ironic, since the Marine Corps is in the most competitive "business" of all—national survival—and is not shy about promoting its training as the world's best.

Training the Best

The Marine Corps takes training very seriously, the cost of failure being so high. The very survival of the nation may depend upon the success of its Marines in battle; the skills they take with them into combat, therefore, must be taught by the finest instructors the country has to offer. Marine Corps drill instructors are just that—America's best. They are carefully screened, experienced professionals who have had to endure not one but two boot camps. D.I. School is offered only to the cream of the Corps, who have demonstrated excellence over and above the already high standard exhibited by their peers. Every D.I., nationwide, is given the same training so that every "boot," no matter where he is, is trained alike. Anyone who has gone through Marine Corps boot camp, as the authors did just out of high school, regards his drill instructor with a mixture of awe, fear, and total respect.

In civilian life, there is a saying that goes, "If you can't do, teach." In the Marine Corps, it is quite the opposite: "If you *can* do, teach."

How many corporations can truly say their training programs are run by the best the company has to offer? All too often, corporate trainers are veteran employees the company doesn't quite know what else to do with. They are not "trained to be trainers," and many are not particularly proud of what they do. There is no master plan to ensure every new hire receives an identical indoctrination, so the instructors end up teaching *their* way, perpetuating a culture that may or may not be in the best interests of the corporation. To underscore their years of experience to the new hires, trainers frequently ridicule company policy and emphasize instead the way the world "really" works, instilling cynicism in the young men and women before them. A Marine Corps D.I. will never, ever, try to elevate his own status among his recruits by criticizing his beloved Corps.

The corporate trainer should feel his job is the most important in the company, because it is. The consequences of poor training in business, while not as dramatic as in the military, are no less fatal to the corporation. The trainer should be, whenever possible, appointed from within the organization. He should be at his prime. Remember: a tour of duty as a drill instructor is the zenith of a Marine's career. If being a teacher is the most important career assignment in the most elite fighting force on the face of the earth, why should it mean less in private enterprise?

Every company has one mission: to prevail in the marketplace. Everything else—providing good jobs, strengthening the community—is secondary to, and dependent upon, victory in the marketplace. Its employees, therefore, must be taught by the best. Top performers in sales, manufacturing, service, and so on should be rewarded by a "tour of duty" as a company instructor. If commission is forfeited, as in the case of salespeople, the company should make up for it. Corporations can take some of the money that is lost every year due to inadequate training and apply it toward doing it right the first time.

Train From a Common Starting Point

If there is one image in the public's imagination that seems to characterize Marine Corps boot camp, it is that of a square-jawed drill instructor shouting into the terrified face of a recruit, who trembles at attention. The general public may not be aware of the other side of the D.I.—the mentoring side—but it is quite right in assuming that there is a lot of yelling going on in boot camp. In fact, there is so much intimidation in the first few weeks that soon each and every recruit has that wide-eyed "deer caught in the headlights" look.

For most recruits, these first few weeks of boot camp represent the greatest shock of their young lives. Those who have come from nurturing, supportive backgrounds—where parents, teachers, and friends have been nice to them—are totally unprepared for the angry faces of the D.I. thrust into their own. Even the tougher recruits, who grew up on the streets, are "scared straight" by the snarling drill instructors. No amount of following orders seems to mollify the D.I., who glares at each recruit as if he had been sent from hell to torment Marine Corps instructors. Of all the challenges posed by boot camp, it is the lack of a friendly face that may be the most disheartening. Even the chaplain is a hard-nose.

Unbeknownst to the recruits, their drill instructor actually has their best interests at heart. The Marine Corps, faced with the nearly impossible task of getting so many disparate individuals to pull in the same direction in only twelve weeks, has no choice but to reduce all to a common denominator. Every head is nearly shaven; first names are sent back home with the civilian clothes; privacy is a thing of the past.

It is in this early stage of boot camp when the Marine Corps most resembles a cult. Recruits look alike, sound alike, and obey instantly. When questioned, they shout out memorized words of the General Orders as if it were part of a sacred text. But the Marine Corps is *not* a cult. Identities are taken away, but only for a short time; the Marine Corps gives them back.

Once everybody is in a receptive state of mind to learn the Marine Corps way, the drill instructors begin to back off a little. They encourage problem solving and initiative. They even mutter a few words of encouragement here and there—words that the recruit will savor throughout the day. As the weeks go by, the D.I. becomes more of a mentor. To some recruits from broken families, he will be the father they never had. By graduation day, the recruits who were wide-eyed automatons two months before have become their own selves, confident, rebuilt, transformed into Marines.

Business managers are faced with challenges that are very

similar to those confronted by the D.I. New employees, from various backgrounds, must learn the company way in a fairly short time—not as short, perhaps, as in boot camp, but the sooner the better. Bad habits must be broken, new skills must be learned; "civilians" at home, the new employees must become corporate soldiers during the day.

Of course, many of the drill instructor's techniques are a bit robust for private enterprise, but the principle of having everyone begin at a common starting point is certainly applicable to a company's "basic training." The opening greeting at the very first class should be: "Forget everything you think you know about the subject. You are going to learn it the right way, the company way."

Even seasoned professionals will allow an instructor to sweep away all previously formed conceptions if he has sufficient authority and a refreshing way of looking at a subject they feel they have already mastered. In fact, even experts enjoy not having to be experts for a while and make use of the experience to fill in the areas in which they are secretly weak. Most new employees, however, are likely to be young and have less "baggage" from previous companies with them. But all must begin at the same starting line.

It is critical that all instructors be reading from the same hymnbook, regardless of how many training facilities a large corporation might have, so that the training is standardized. Every instructor must be earnest. Why is it so many of them feel compelled to demonstrate their own expertise by openly questioning the very techniques they are teaching?

Tell Them They're Elite, Over and Over Again

Not all Marines are six-foot-four-inch muscular hulks. In fact, since the Corps is composed of a cross-section of humanity, most Marines are of average height and weight. People are often surprised, while watching news footage of the Marines "hitting the beach" to see gawky eighteen-year-olds who seem barely able to keep their helmets from slipping down over their faces. What makes these Marines different from other gawky eighteen-year-olds is that they *feel* like six-foot-four-inch muscular hulks.

From Day One at boot camp—even before, in the recruiting office—the young recruit is told that he will soon be a member of the greatest fighting organization on the face of the earth. A hundred times a day, from every mouth that speaks, he hears how special he is. His longing for graduation is not simply a longing for the day when the harsh rigors of boot camp end, but a longing for the day when he will officially be one of "The Few, the Proud," "The World's Finest," "The First to Fight," "The Leathernecks," and so on. By the time he graduates, the new Marine is convinced, not of his own valor, perhaps, but of the legendary valor of the organization to which he now belongs.

There is something to be said for constant positive reinforcement. If Marine Corps boot camp could somehow be experimentally duplicated, but without the incessant self-aggrandizement, it would be interesting to see what kind of individual emerged. Surely, he would be in great physical shape. But the critical mental factor would be missing. One could expect a graduating class of young men who could do more push-ups than they could before beginning training, but not a tightly knit organization whose members are willing to die for one another.

Not only does the Marine Corps convince its own members of its uniqueness; it persuades the general public as well. Phrases like "Tell it to the Marines," or "Send in the Marines" have become a kind of nationally recognized shorthand for describing the seriousness of a situation. The Marine Corps is aware of its formidable reputation, but it does not rest upon its laurels. The public relations effort never stops. It must be said, of course, that this kind of shameless self-promotion is based on historical fact; the Marines can back up what they say. It's just that they are not shy about saying it.

Over the years, an unshakable conviction has developed. The Marines believe they are the best; the American public believes it; the world at large believes it. About the only people who don't believe it are the elite, secretive special forces of the army and the navy—the Green Berets and the Seals—who are even fewer and even prouder than the Marines but who have never caught the imagination of the American public precisely because they are so secretive. Most young men do not want to join an ultrasecret force of American ninjas; they want to be Marines and they want everybody to know it.

And that is one of the reasons for the incessant PR. The Marines require forty thousand new members every year, so they must constantly recruit. It is also good policy to remind the enemies of America that the Marine Corps is ready to strike at a moment's notice anywhere in the world. More than a few terrorist regimes have suddenly become full of love and kindness when American Marines have hovered overhead in helicopters. If scientists were to discover life on other planets, the Marine Corps would probably broadcast its message into space.

The business community can learn much from the self-promoting effort of the Marine Corps. A company must first make its own employees "believers," then the public, then the competition.

All employees—factory workers, administrative personnel, and sales associates—must be made to believe that their product and services are the best in the industry. Internal demonstrations should be held in front of the assembled company personnel to explain why their product is made the way it is. Competitive products should be compared, side by side, so that everyone knows to some degree the features and benefits of their own handiwork. Competitive rhetoric should be examined for its veracity so that every employee has an answer to the claims made by others. There should be no doubt in the mind of everybody on the payroll that the company produces the best value for the dollar in the marketplace.

Companies cannot be shy about self-aggrandizing promotional campaigns. They should run advertisements in praise of themselves. Product and marketing announcements should be sent to the local newspapers; these press releases should then be distributed throughout the rank and file of the organization, as if to say, "Look what the papers are saying about us." Every company should have a beautiful Web site on the Internet, chock full of self-serving statements, production information, organization history, and so on. Internally, newsletters should be put out on a frequent basis, replete with employee profiles, commendations, and good news "from the front" (e.g., major sales, happy customers). Every opportunity must be taken to broadcast an achievement. Management must infect its personnel with enthusiasm, because, if it doesn't happen at that level, it may not happen in the mind of the customer.

We are not suggesting a propaganda machine for its own sake. A company must, like the Marines, be able to back up its claims of quality and performance. But, like the Marines, it must keep on trumpeting its own horn—to attract the best employees, to remind the public of the benefits of the product, and to strike fear in the hearts of the competition.

Teach Leadership in Little Steps

The Marine Corps believes that leaders are made, not born. Of course, they have to believe this; the supply of "born leaders" would be far too unpredictable. In combat, fire team leaders, squad leaders, platoon commanders, and company commanders can be killed in battle and must be replaced on the spot. Their replacements, in turn, may be killed and need to be replaced. Leaders, therefore, must be cranked out of boot camp and officer candidate school in large numbers. Fortunately for the nation, the Marine Corps has the formula for cultivating leadership qualities in even the most unlikely individuals.

A recruit going through basic training learns how to lead by degrees. His first command may be as menial as taking responsibility for picking up the cigarette butts on the barracks grounds. The next step along the path to leadership might be marching first a squad of twelve across the parade grounds, later, a platoon of fifty, then a company of two hundred. To the recruit, leadership is only a stripe away, visible and achievable. The desire to lead is created through a course of progressive resistance, where every additional burden is incremental, until the mature Marine is prepared to take on the ultimate leadership challenge—a combat command.

The corporation that prepares its leaders, whether shift supervisors or CEOs, through similar "baby steps" will have lower turnover and fewer disappointments. But, all too often, the expectations of the board of directors and management are brutally high. The corporate culture is in some ways more macho and unforgiving than even that in the military. Individuals are expected to take charge immediately; if they are unable to do so, management will find somebody who can. Many a career could have flowered, at great savings to the corporation, had management taken the time to build a solid leadership foundation incrementally.

Of course, each future leader within the organization must be cultivated on an individual basis. Management has to have the sensitivity to treat each employee in ways that will elicit the proper response. Even drill instructors, for all their bluster, watch each recruit with a keen eye, recognizing who may need a little more discipline and who could be motivated more effectively with a pat on the back.

And, like the D.I., the manager must have a plan he strictly abides by. He mustn't allow the fluctuating demands of business, with all of its "fires" to be put out, to interfere with the process of leadership cultivation. If an employee has been told that, on Monday, he will be introduced to a new responsibility or task, that schedule should be kept. If adhered to, the plan will take care of itself; before he knows it, an employee will be standing before him with a confidence and an eagerness to serve that he will find almost unrecognizable.

Cultivate, Rather Than "Weed Out"

Every twelve weeks, the drill instructor stares at a batch of new recruits from all walks of life. He can tell at a glance that some young men seem to have more potential than others, while some recruits seem hopelessly without potential. The D.I.'s mission is to bring each and every individual up to the standard of excellence demanded by the Marine Corps. The D.I. will chew out, harass, and punish the platoon "screwup," but he will never give up on him. A recruit who has a difficult time of it may be sent to the Motivational Platoon (a.k.a. the Fat Farm), or even go through boot camp twice. But eventually he will emerge from the process a Marine. The Marine Corps doesn't weed out; it cultivates.

Corporations, on the other hand, have little patience with incompetence. While there may be more tolerance today, for fear of litigation, management generally writes off the nonproductive employee and looks for ways to get rid of him. The weeding-out process is a costly one. Every employee, including newly hired ones, represents an investment. It costs the company to hire and train new employees, and it costs again for his replacement, who in turn may have to be replaced. Turnover can be significantly reduced if management and the human resources department, like the D.I., work with and develop their problem associates. Even if they fail to transform these employees, they have, by making every attempt, strengthened the company's case should it be challenged later.

"Height Works"

In addition to the Rappelling Tower, where recruits learn the skills necessary to descend a simulated helicopter line down a sheer fifty-foot wall, there are numerous other very high obstacle course structures that have a less practical application. "They're primarily confidence builders," explains one drill instructor, Staff Sergeant Rodney Lowe. "I used to shake in my boots up there, but once I got over it, I felt like I could do anything. Height really works."

Staff Sergeant Lowe turns to the big sign on the field. It is hard to imagine him ever shaking in his boots. "You see," he says, pointing, "that's why the sign says 'Confidence Course,' instead of 'Obstacle Course.' "

What do towering, confidence-building structures on a military base have to do with management training for private enterprise? Are we suggesting that aspiring corporate leaders be put through an obstacle—that is, a "confidence"—course of their own? Well, yes and no.

We are not suggesting that men and women be encouraged to climb fifty-foot ladders, or even walk across a plank between two desks. Managers could be sent off to self-reliance programs such as Outward Bound, to offload some of the liability, but the Marine Corps's confidence course principles can be practiced in-house.

"Height" can be used in a metaphorical sense, forcing one to rise above his or her station. In leadership "boot camps," managers could, for example, be assigned role-play positions well above their current job titles. A factory shift supervisor can be given the role of a vice president of manufacturing who is forced to increase production, or to downsize. A sales manager could be "appointed" CEO and have to find the proper balance between volume sales and profit. A CEO could be promoted for a day to the position of a chairman of the board of directors who must explain to the stockholders the need to take the step into the international market. After successfully managing the responsibilities of a much higher level, one may find one's own responsibilities less overwhelming.

"Height," in a literal sense, affords a panoramic view of the scene below. And so do heightened responsibilities. Individuals who participate in these kinds of role-play exercises will find their own awareness has been expanded, as has their appreciation of the challenges faced by others within the organization.

Take Advantage of the Magic of Simulation

From the obstacle course where the sound of rapid-fire machine guns deafen the ear, to million-dollar jet cockpits that never leave the ground, the Marine Corps believes in simulation. The theory is, if the training is realistic enough, the subconscious mind accepts it as real experience. The philosophy is summed up in the boot camp motto, "The more you sweat in peace, the less you bleed in war." Indeed, the training of the elite forces, such as the Marine Corps' Force Recon, the army's Green Berets, and the navy's Seals, is so realistic that there are occasional, and regrettable, fatalities.

There are many Marines today who have never seen combat. Prior to Desert Storm, the number was even higher. Thankfully, there has not been a lot of combat in the world that has involved the United States to require the mobilization of a force of 170,000. Of course, one of the reasons this country is not involved is due to the extreme readiness of the Marine Corps, which tends to make rogue nations think twice before antagonizing Uncle Sam. Actual combat experience, however, is unnecessary if the training is sufficiently realistic. And Marine Corps training is so realistic that all who go through it are, at a subconscious level, "veterans." The saying "You fight like you train" has been proven time and time again.

Through simulation, one can become an "expert" in something he has never actually done. The best example of this is the Apollo astronauts, who were all highly trained experts in something nobody had ever done—landing on the moon. As they were sent literally into the unknown, all of their surroundings were reassuringly familiar. The "actual" spacecraft console was identical to the simulated one. The "actual" operations had been performed thousands of times before, in a cockpit that never left the ground. The astronauts were "veterans" at what they were doing, even though it was their first time. In fact, news reporters were disappointed by the interviews with the returning explorers. When asked, "What was it like landing on the moon?," they responded, "It was just like the drills we've been doing for years."

Every corporation should have a Top Gun sales school in which new hires are put through realistic sales and negotiating situations to prepare them for the "outside." A salesperson who has encountered every plausible objection in training and who has been taught to respond will be less taken aback when faced with resistance in the real world of commerce. Many companies have invested in top-gun schools where their sales forces are videotaped and evaluated as they deal with a trainer portraying a "customer from Hell." As in the case of military training, the tougher the simulation, the more capable the graduate.

Encourage Peer Pressure

Basic training in the Marine Corps does not always seem fair. Recruits are sometimes yelled at for things they didn't do. A drill instructor, frustrated by not finding anything wrong during a barracks inspection, may grab a pillow off a bunk, throw it on the gleaming floor, and demand to know why there's a pillow on the floor. But nothing seems more unfair to the average recruit than the way the D.I. reacts to the "screwups."

If a recruit just can't seem to get it right—drilling, shooting, or spit-shining his boots—the rest of the platoon, not the offender, will be ordered to the ground for knuckle pushups. If a recruit does not keep pace on a run, those who finished on time are punished. If he drops his rifle, the rest of his comrades will pay the price, not the one who was careless. The authors remember an incident from their boot camp experience, in which three recruits who had the misfortune of not qualifying on the rifle range were made to sit in lounge chairs and drink tall glasses of lemonade while the rest of the forty-five members of the platoon, who all did well on the rifle range, were put through an endless series of exercises beneath the hot sun.

Punishing those who did it right for the actions of those who did it wrong may strike us as a hellish, reverse morality. But there is a method to the madness. The young Marines are learning the hard way that the mistake of one man can affect the entire unit. In combat, everybody may pay for the mistake of only one single individual.

Secondly, the D.I.s are encouraging peer pressure of the

most persuasive sort. The hapless "screwup" finds himself confronted after hours with some very impatient comrades, who will show him, in no uncertain terms, how to drill, reassemble his rifle, and so on. In extreme cases, "blanket parties" may be held in the middle of the night. The following morning, the recruit may show up for reveille with a black eye and a brand new attitude. Of course, blanket parties are strictly forbidden by today's Marine Corps, but it is safe to say that peer pressure still plays an integral role in the building of a Marine.

How can a business leader instill a similar, albeit kinder and gentler, culture of peer pressure to deal with his own "screwups"? One method is to promote contests requiring a 100 percent compliance in order to win. For example, you can treat an entire factory shift to a special catered lunch, "on the house," provided that there have been no safety violations of any kind for thirty days. Since all violations must be documented, the vast majority of conscientious workers will soon learn why there is to be no special lunch this month. This is not to suggest that management should try to create vigilantism within the organization. Private enterprise equivalents of blanket parties can be avoided if the "good" employees are provided with a mechanism to communicate their concerns to the "bad" employees.

Team meetings can be held on a monthly basis, without the presence of management, during which the troublesome employee can be confronted with the consequences of his actions. The team can make it clear that they are all being punished—or at least, not being rewarded—because of his irresponsible behavior. Even the most cynical individual will be affected by a united front of fellow employees.

Set Up Warrior Stations

Each confidence course event of The Crucible—the fifty-four hour ordeal all recruits must go through in the last week of training—is followed by a "warrior station, " which may be nothing more than a few logs poking out of the bleak landscape, representing yet another challenge to the exhausted recruits. Warrior stations are unique in that they are designed around an actual heroic feat performed by a Marine at some point in the nation's history.

Before each station, a simple redwood post displays a weather-worn black and white photograph of the Marine in whose honor that particular warrior station is named. The recruits stand before the photo while one of them reads the inscription aloud, describing the brave deed performed. Then they reenact the very deed, symbolically. For example, in the Warrior Station called Garcia's Leap, named in honor of a Marine who leapt from rigging to rigging during a naval battle in 1812 so that he could continue to fire down upon the enemy, each recruit stands on a stump and jumps out toward a dangling rope, just slightly out of reach. Below, his comrades are poised to catch him. The recruit, who cannot reach the rope by design, bellyflops into the arms of his buddies.

The drill instructor is the first to go. Even he cannot reach the dangling rope and falls into the arms of the recruits he has been screaming at for the past two and half months. Interestingly, this is the first time the recruits have touched their D.I. They cradle him in their arms for a moment, in effect supporting their leader. Then each man makes the leap, with the same results, each being cradled by his comrades.

At the end of each Warrior Station, all huddle together in a semicircle, headed by the D.I. He is now almost totally in his role as mentor. Soft spoken, he asks questions of each recruit about Garcia's heroic actions. Exhausted, they are, ironically, more receptive to the lessons to be learned from another exhausted Marine who, in 1812, pushed himself beyond his limitations.

The Warrior Stations are brilliantly conceived (by Marines, not outsourced psychologists) to serve as learning platforms and as transition points in the recruit's relations with his drill instructor. No longer a fire-breathing dragon, he has become a mentor. The recruits will still jump at the sound of his voice, to be sure, but they are no longer afraid to approach him with a personal problem.

Businesses should introduce the warrior station concept into their basic training. The comparatively "heroic" deeds of salespeople, negotiators, or product innovators who have shown great initiative and team work should be discussed, thought about, and symbolically reenacted. Any company more than a few years old simply has to have some praiseworthy examples of salesmanship, managerial skills on the production line, or waste-cutting brainstorms, or it wouldn't be in business. In an older, established company, there are hundreds of inspirational "war stories" that sit on the shelf like books that are never read. An honorable legacy is allowed to gather dust, never to be passed on to the new generation of employees.

How many associates of a large corporation know anything of the biography of their CEO? In the Marines, even privates have heard stories about "the old man," and they respect him all the more for it. CEOs also have histories, sometimes very colorful and inspiring histories, but, for whatever reason, the war stories and anecdotes are never shared with the rank and file. "Warrior stations" during employee training would correct this unforgivable modesty on the part of corporate leaders and their managers. Past successes would be studied and appreciated, not forgotten.

Even exercises such as Garcia's Leap would be appropriate. Imagine the psychological effect of a sales manager leaping from his desk into the waiting arms of the people he must depend upon to make quota. Imagine their reactions as they momentarily cradle their leader. Yes, there would be comic potential and perhaps a lot of self-consciousness, but the message of interdependency would be learned at a physical level, which is much more memorable than the intellectual level.

Throughout boot camp, recruits hear constant stories of why the Marines are the elite branch of America's armed forces. The study of the Marine Corps Manual, with its detailed historical accounts, is augmented by war stories from the D.I. himself. By graduation day, every recruit is fully aware that he belongs to a very special organization with a record he does not want to tarnish. There is no reason why corporate trainers cannot tell "war stories" of their own, recalling past business triumphs. The new hire should enter the competitive marketplace fully armed with a sense of his company's history, including business deals won by his predecessors, innovations that redefined the industry, and presentations that swept the customers off their feet.

"Temper" Fidelis

Certainly one of the most enduring Hollywood images of Marine Corps boot camp is that of a drill instructor screaming into the ear of a terrified recruit. Unlike most Hollywood clichés, this one is quite accurate. The D.I. will harass, ridicule, and chew out a recruit in front of the entire platoon. On occasion, one screaming D.I. will attract another, so that the hapless recruit may have to confront two or three furiously angry faces. But, oddly enough, the recruit is not embarrassed; he has heard his D.I. chew out everybody else as well. Furthermore, he knows that the D.I. is much more bark than bite and that the dressing down he is enduring will go no further. His mistakes are not entered into his service record, nor are they brought to the attention of an officer. The drill instructor, for all his verbal abuse, has no intention of throwing the recruit out of the Marine Corps. On the contrary, he will build the recruit into a full-fledged Marine.

Corporate management is much more unforgiving, in its own quiet way. Employees are not often chastised by a good, old-fashioned "talking to." Instead, they are taken into a private room with the supervisor and a representative from HR. The supervisor does not raise his voice; he simply enters the offense into the personnel record of the employee. The incident, instead of being frankly discussed, resolved, and forgotten, is forever remembered.

Management could learn a lot from the Marine Corps D.I. There is something to be said about chewing out an employee, then letting it end there. Most people will accept criticism if it is for their own good and if it is possible to make up for the offense by good behavior. But management is often so intent on documenting every grievance, to build a case for possible termination down the line, that the employee feels branded.

Utilize Remote Training Facilities

Marine Corps boot camp, like Hades, is not only a mythical experience; it is a place. Recruits must travel to it; they do not begin basic training in the same office where they signed on the dotted line. Once the bus passes through the famous gates of the training depots at San Diego or Parris Island, the recruit enters a world unto itself. Other than by way of mail, all communication with the outside is cut off; no newspapers or radios are allowed. Even communication with the "inside" world is restricted—recruits can't even speak to each other most of the time. The conditions, while monastic, are ideal for learning. The "boot" eats, lives, and breathes his training, without interruption or distraction—which is why so much is accomplished in the twelve short weeks of boot camp. One can only imagine just how long the transformation from recruit to Marine would take—if it would even occur—were the recruit to be allowed to go "off campus" for lunch and sleep at home every night.

Companies have much less than twelve weeks to indoctrinate their newly hired associates. Whatever they can do to isolate the trainee from outside distractions will help accelerate the process. A separate, remote facility dedicated exclusively to training is clearly the best way to begin. The new employee, away from home and stuck in class, is much more likely to focus on the subject matter at hand than one who is allowed to live two lives—his company's and his own—for the week or two of basic training. Remote educational facilities are also impressive investments, ones that speak of the company's stability and commitment. Just being there tends to create an obligation to reciprocate.

If it is not possible for the company to maintain a separate training facility, office space must be set aside with all the trappings of a classroom. The more a company can dignify its training facility, however humble, the greater the value the new employee will place in his training. Institutionalized learning environments return us to our school days—an earnest time of life for most of us. With the possible exception of planting ivy on the walls, the company should create the appearance of an educational setting. The trainees should be kept as isolated as possible for the entire day, which of course rules out arbitrary phone calls, faxes, and beepers. And the trainers, themselves, must share the isolation; D.I.s, after all, live with their recruits, night and day, for twelve weeks. The company may even want to sequester the class, like a jury, in a local hotel, where the students dine together with a different company executive every night. Two weeks of such intensity will create an alumnus. The "graduates" will have a common, worthwhile reference point throughout their careers.

Invest in Training in Multiple Applications

Unique to Marine Corps basic training is its emphasis on exposing each recruit to scenarios he may never encounter and to weapons he may never fire again. Of course, one would expect every Marine to be proficient with a rifle; even if he is destined to be a cook, he is first and foremost a rifleman. But beyond that, every recruit has hands-on classes in weapons that only a very few will actually specialize in—rocket launchers, recoilless rifles, artillery pieces, explosives, and heavy machine guns—on the assumption that in the chaos of combat he should be able to take over for a wounded Marine, regardless of his specialty. He is also shown the fundamentals of other skills, such as field radio operation, first aid, and engine repair, so that he may be of some use when the "expert" has not arrived or has become a casualty.

In the corporate environment, where the occasional case of flu is the most serious casualty, there is no need to back up each employee with a replacement. Individuals are recruited and trained for a specific job, and, if the need arises, a "temp" may be brought in to fill a sudden gap. But the Marine Corps' principle of training in multiple applications is a sound one and should be considered by every business.

When a new employee is exposed, during his "basic training," to duties he was not specifically hired for, his own responsibilities become clearer. A sales trainee, for example, who spends time in Order Entry, personally trying to decipher some of the paperwork sent in by salespeople who had to make a deadline, will gain an appreciation for the kinds of problems that department has to deal with; perhaps his own paperwork will benefit from the experience. The same trainee, sent to the factory floor or to the assembly line, will see with his own eyes the quality control enforced by the company. A couple of days spent in the field with service personnel will further increase his confidence; he is providing not only the best product but the best service in the industry, as well. Time spent with the Research and Development department and the on-line Customer Help Desk, in Shipping, MIS, and Installation, will make a true believer out of him. The difference between him and a salesperson from the competition who has been trained only in sales "closing" techniques will be apparent to the customer.

There are times, too, when a fundamental knowledge of the duties of others has a practical application. In 1997, a union strike against UPS threatened to paralyze commerce throughout the nation. For two weeks, the nightly news programs showed clips of UPS managers donning the famous uniform, loading and driving the big brown trucks themselves. Although their efforts were largely symbolic, these managers demonstrated a competence that will not be forgotten by the returning employees, many of whom expressed a grudging respect.

Delay Official Recognition

It takes three months of arduous training before a recruit is finally called a Marine. During those months, the recruit sustains himself through the knuckle pushups and endless "double-time" marches up and down the hills by repeating the mantra "I want to be a Marine" over and over again. Isolated from all the distractions of society, he finds that time passes very slowly in boot camp, as in jail, and the day when he will be called *Marine* seems very far off indeed.

But it does finally come, at the very end of The Crucible, which explains why the recruits who have endured fifty-four sleepless hours of the most strenuous activity can, nonetheless, race up the final hundred yards of Grim Reaper. This is the day they will be officially recognized as Marines.

The delayed gratification creates an almost unbearable suspense in the mind of the recruit, which further elevates the training period in his mind. Just imagine if boot camp were to begin with this greeting: "Welcome, Marines." The term itself would be worthless. The authors remember, from their boot camp experience in the early 1960s, being addressed as "Maggot" for three full months, until graduation day. When we first heard the word *Marine*, we thought our D.I. was speaking to someone else. When we finally realized that the grinning drill instructor was talking to us, as fellow Marines, the sense of achievement, and of gratitude for being accepted, made us inarticulate with joy.

There is absolutely no reason why a forward-thinking corporation could not make use of this concept of delayed gratification for all incoming employees. The initial two to three months of employment should be thought of as an evaluation period—for both sides. Even if he is assured by colleagues that the term is only perfunctory and that "promotion" to the status of full-fledged employee is virtually automatic, there is still that element of doubt, the fear that he may be the exception. It goes without saying that Graduation Day, when it comes, must be sufficiently rewarding. The new associate should feel the same sense of achievement and, yes, of gratitude that new Marines experience at their graduation.

The notion that an employee should feel privileged to work for a company may sound outrageously naive to many employers, who are currently involved in the bidding war for today's graduating "whiz kids." It is quite true that highly qualified college grads have their pick of major companies and are courted much like PAC Ten athletes. But it is also true that the other branches of the armed forces promise much more in the way of material benefits (e.g., $40,000 toward a college education) than the Marine Corps. The Marines, however, consider it a privilege to belong to the close-knit organization of the Corps and conduct themselves accordingly. True, the Corps does miss a few "big catches," but the quality of the young men and women who are attracted by the uncompromising, elitist attitude of the Marines more than makes up for it. The corporation can confidently emulate this attitude, if it, like the Marine Corps, can back it up with performance.

Make Everyone Go Through Your "Basic Training"

Each Marine, regardless of job specialty or duty station, shares with every other Marine on the face of the earth at least one essential experience—boot camp. They have, of course, much more in common, including the fact that every Marine is a rifleman first, but there are many roads to take in the Corps, in terms of both specialty and tours of duty, and Marines will have careers as varied as those available in civilian life. The one common point of contact for everyone who wears, or has worn, a Marine Corps uniform is that each of them has had to endure the most rigorous basic training in the world—Marine Corps boot camp.

There are only two Marine Corps boot camps in existence—Marine Corps Recruiting Depot at Parris Island, South Carolina, and MCRD at San Diego (officer's candidate school in Quantico, Virginia, though even tougher than Parris Island and MCRD, is not considered a "boot camp" for the rank and file). Graduates of the East or West Coast boot camps predictably believe their experience to have been the toughest. Parris Island graduates call those who went through MCRD in San Diego "Hollywood Marines." San Diego graduates point out all the mountains they have had to "hump," noting that Parris Island is as flat as a pancake. To add fuel to the fire, those who attended boot camp "in the old days" (i.e., whenever *they* went) predictably describe their experience as hell on earth.

The truth is, of course, that both boot camps are equally tough. The recruits themselves, having no choice on the matter (those from the eastern half of the nation are sent to Parris Island; those from the western half go to San Diego), find the challenges of either boot camp to be more than they bargained for. And that is the basis for the respect Marines feel for each other: every Marine knows his comrade went through the same ordeal he himself had to endure. With that respect comes a certain comfort level; he knows the man wearing the uniform next to him, friend or stranger, can be depended upon. Every Marine is a proven entity, at least in that one important sense; he has successfully undergone a tremendous test of character. And every Marine he will ever meet, without exception, will have gone through it, as well.

Just as the common bond of a shared ordeal unites all Marines, a shared experience among employees, if it is sufficiently demanding, can create a similar sense of mutual respect. One can see it in any company: employees who have "come up through the ranks" together enjoy higher esteem among themselves than, say, the boss's nephew, who joined the organization right out of college. Of course, the boss's nephew may be capable of earning the respect of his peers, but it would be an easier row to hoe if he were put through the same "basic training" as everyone else.

Of course, new employee training and indoctrination in private enterprise will not be as intense as Marine Corps boot camp, but it should enjoy a reputation within the industry as the best training to be had. A company's basic school should have many of the elements of boot camp: it should be difficult—with assignments, tasks, and role plays that simultaneously terrify and bring out the best in each student—and rewarding, so that every graduate is both relieved and inspired. And everyone must be put through it, instructors as well as new hires.

Inculcate a Defining Moment in Your "Basic Training"

Marine Corps officer training has always been as tough as—some enlisted men say tougher than—boot camp for the rank and file. This is as it should be, since the officer must lead the pace, not simply keep up with his men. For years Officer Candidate School was capped by an especially difficult final two-and-a-half-day ordeal, in which the prospective officers endured sleep and food deprivation while going through a seemingly endless number of obstacles and field exercises. The current commandant of the Marine Corps, Charles Krulak, upon taking command took this concept of a final, defining ordeal and applied it to basic training for all Marines.

As of 1996, every Marine recruit must complete not only the legendary rigors of boot camp but the even more demanding fifty-four-hour test of character called The Crucible, as well. With enough food in their packs for one meal, the recruits begin the series of challenges heartily enough. But, after a couple of sleepless days and nights climbing hills, crawling through mud, and shivering in their field jackets, the "fog of war" sets in, and they begin to feel some of the disorientation and mental stress they will encounter in combat.

Every challenge they face is ingeniously designed so that success is possible only if they work as a team. If all but one recruit manages to complete an event within the time constraints, they have all failed. The team must get through as a unit. The drill instructors, who are with their men every step of the way, are particularly "hands off" during this period, forcing the recruits to think for themselves. Since there is no one way to solve the puzzle of each event, the D.I.s are pleasantly surprised by the creativity employed by the recruits to complete the event as a whole.

This emphasis on problem solving often brings out other surprises. Recruits who have been timid thus far into boot camp, seeing that nothing seems to be working and that the time is running out, now step forward with ideas of their own. Their drill instructors are often amazed to see the transformation. Equally impressive is the evidence of teamwork. Those who have trouble keeping up with the pace are helped by their comrades. Food is shared; words of encouragement are whispered to one another; the team is becoming part of the tightly knit entity that is the Corps.

The fifty-four-hour Crucible ends with an exhausting forced march and a private, internal graduation. The authors were privileged to attend this ceremony at Camp Pendleton. The troops, hidden by the mountains and valleys that have made Camp Pendleton infamous, could be heard miles away singing cadence. As the column of two hundred men approached Grim Reaper, which seemed to us like a mountain peak, they broke into a run. Led by their officers and D.I.s, they literally charged up the hill while wearing fifty pounds of combat gear.

The men were then assembled on the top of the hill, where they stood at attention, chests heaving. After a flag-raising ceremony and a congratulatory speech by their company commander, the drill instructors, who also hadn't slept for fifty-four hours, walked through the ranks and personally presented each of their recruits with the coveted globe and anchor, signifying their entry into the Corps family. This simple act, accompanied by a few quiet words to each young man, was so moving emotionally that tears streaked the dusty, exhausted, and unashamed faces of 90 percent of the recruits. Even the rough and tough D.I.s had to clear their throats as they looked each recruit in the eye, gripped hands, and addressed him for the first time as "Marine."

Although the recruits would, one week later, parade smartly in clean, pressed uniforms before family and friends during a public ceremony, the private graduation in fatigues will be the one they remember.

Any business that prides itself on its training programs should consider a similar defining experience, which requires the utmost in initiative and creativity from its students. The endurance factor should not be ignored. The Marines keep the recruits awake for fifty-four hours to simulate the stress of war. Future production supervisors and sales managers can certainly be asked to stay up for an "all-nighter" during intensive training exercises (they probably have done so in college many times, during finals).

Technical trainees can be assigned a simulated emergency that must be resolved in two or three days. The solution must require input from everybody on the team. Sales trainees could be given a complex Request For Proposal, with detailed, point-by-point questions that must be answered to the satisfaction of the customer. The exercise could involve both groups, requiring salespeople to work in concert with the "techies" to prepare an integrated, comprehensive presentation before upper management, representing the customer. Intensive negotiations or last-minute redesigns could add realistic stress— the "fog of war." Whatever shape it takes, the exercise must be an experience the participants will always remember. It must be the stuff of reunions

Basic Training—Setting the Standard

Marine Corps basic training is more than the assimilation of numerous skills; it is a rite of passage. There is absolutely no reason why business training could not have just as much dramatic effect on those who go through it. Properly invested in, in terms of both resources and belief, it is possible for a company's "basic training" program to develop such a reputation within the industry that it becomes a credential in itself.

Leadership Strategies Checklist

—Upgrade corporate training so that it becomes an industry-wide credential.

—Reward top performers with a "tour of duty" as a company trainer.

—Train all personnel from a common starting point.

—Constantly remind the employees that they are something special.

—Build leadership capacity incrementally.

—Cultivate, rather than weed out.

—Implement role-play seminars where responsibilities are greatly increased.

—Create "real" experience through realistic simulation training.

—Recognize peer pressure as a management tool.

—Re-enact symbolically the company's past successes.

—Remember that sometimes a "chewing out" is better than a quiet entry into the personnel record.

—Isolate the trainee, and the trainer, from outside distractions.

—Expose the trainee to responsibilities outside his position.

—Delay official recognition, so as to increase its value.

—Require all associates to go through "basic training."

—Institute the Crucible concept: the defining moment of transition from trainee to associate.

3

Supervision: Leading the Rank and File

"Strive to create discipline in yourself and your Marines. Encourage high morale, foster spirit, and train for efficiency. You may never win the Medal of Honor, you may never be cited for your outstanding example, but you will have an inner satisfaction that comes only to those that give their all. Then, if you listen carefully . . . you will hear the voices of all the other good Marines who have gone before whisper the greatest commendation of them all—'Well done, Marine.'"

—Corporal Gary C. Cooper
(Marine Manual FMFM 1–0)

"The Marine Corps taught me to have a plan every day, but to be flexible enough to adjust to the dynamics of the battlefield. I learned that one never goes into battle being led by committee. Today, I impress upon my people the necessity of having goals and the need to measure the progress on a weekly, monthly, and semi-annual basis. I always sit down with my subordinates to track their progress—while applying the same standards to myself."

—Doug Hamlin, Vice President of
Motor Trend, formerly Captain, USMC

The Marine Corps sergeant is a legendary character. Portrayed in fiction and in the movies as a human incarnation of the Marine Corps' mascot—a bulldog—the "sarge" has taken his place in the public's imagination. He epitomizes the gruff, occasionally sentimental caretaker of American youth in uniform. He prepares our children for battle in basic training, leads them into combat whenever the order is given, and watches with a fatherly eye during the normal course of military life. He is loved and appreciated by the nation—but grossly typecast.

The tough but lovable "sarge" of the movies is, in reality, a highly trained professional whose leadership skills should be the envy of any corporation. A Marine Corps noncommissioned officer could walk into the most sophisticated organization in private enterprise and size it up immediately. His abilities to inspire and direct the personnel under his authority would bring credit to any company in any industry. Upper management would do well to examine the successful leadership principles developed and refined by today's Marine Corps noncommissioned officer.

The Credibility of the NCO

The Marine Corps NCO enjoys the respect of his men, in part because they know that he is qualified, having come up through the ranks. The promotional path is open to all, but all who travel must go step by step. A private may work his way up through private first class, lance corporal, corporal, sergeant, staff sergeant, gunnery sergeant, master sergeant, and, finally, sergeant major, but he can never skip a rank. Each position carries its own pay-rate, which is determined by time in grade. Because there are no shortcuts through the ranks and all applicants must meet objective standards, there is a general faith in the validity of the promotion process. The private knows that his sergeant is entitled to "walk the walk" and is not an impostor with three stripes on his sleeve because of a rich uncle.

In the corporation, however, promotional standards are often totally subjective. A person "from the outside" can be arbitrarily put into a position for which he has no direct experience, causing resentment within the ranks. Salaries can vary out of all proportion to time in grade, and morale within the company often suffers because someone has peeked at another's paycheck. Corporations would do well to standardize the promotional and pay requirements so that achievement is possible to all and sidestepping is possible to no one.

In the Marines, the NCO who isn't revered is the exception. In many corporations, the supervisor who *is* revered is the exception.

The NCO Is Proud of His Roots

The Marine Corps noncommissioned officer may be in the middle of the organizational structure, that is, between the officers and the ranks, but he is much more closely identified with the ranks. NCOs live, train, and fight with their troops, sharing the same risks and deprivations. The only outward symbols of the NCO's authority (besides his obvious confidence) are the stripes on his sleeve; otherwise his uniform is identical to that of a private. He is an integral part of the team, without being "one of the boys." He is a leader, but one who gets just as cold and wet on maneuvers as the men he leads. He is an "enlisted man" and proud of it.

The culture of the Marine Corps has a lot to do with the NCO's self-esteem. He is constantly reminded of the history of the Corps and of the noncommissioned officers who have been immortalized in Marine Corps history. He walks on streets and past buildings named after privates, corporals, and sergeants who have received the Medal of Honor. Out on the parade field, he watches the official "teacher" in the Marine Corps—an NCO drill instructor—put future officers through their paces. Wherever he goes, he can see the admiration in the eyes of the young recruits. And, as he salutes a Marine officer, the officer will always return the salute. (One of the legends every NCO has heard tells of a young officer who did not return an enlisted man's salute—and was subsequently ordered by the renowned Marine general Chesty Puller to stand there and salute the nervous private one hundred times.)

In the corporate workplace, many who come from the lower levels of the organization are eager to disavow their origins. What is the first thing a factory line operator does, upon his promotion to shift supervisor? He comes to work the very next morning in a white shirt and tie, thereby identifying himself with management. When he eats lunch, it will be with his new friends in management. Instead of being proud of his roots, he sheds the telltale uniform of his past and tries to associate himself with what he perceives to be the upper class within the company. Indeed, the higher he goes up the corporate ladder, the more distant the memory of his days on the assembly line become. More often than not, this kind of behavior costs him the respect of the most important layer of the organization—the workforce.

The corporate culture is not obligated to reflect the culture of the world outside; the company can create a better one of its own. Just because society in general places managers above factory assemblers, it does not follow that the assembler must report to a workplace that gives the same message. A young Marine private, sitting at a train station, may watch the businessmen in expensive suits walk by and experience a pang of inequality, but the second he steps onto a Marine Corps base he feels ten feet tall—because his organization holds him in the highest esteem. The corporation that exalts the backbone of the company—those on the "front lines"—and provides its workers with the sharpest uniforms, the cleanest, safest workplace, the most prominent awards for achievement, and managers who exist for them, will create a culture from which the assembler will be in no hurry to disassociate himself.

Balance Management With "Mustangs"

In Officer Candidate School, unlike boot camp, the aspiring officer can drop out of the program whenever he wishes. And many do. The attrition rate is as high as 25 percent, which should not be surprising, considering that OCS is even more strenuous than boot camp. It is a lot to ask of a college graduate whose life experiences have not been particularly toughening. Marine Corps Officer Candidate School is extremely difficult, mentally and physically, because those who graduate will be expected to lead men who consider themselves to be as tough as nails. The officer must be able to do everything they can do, and more. A combat command is incredibly demanding. The training, therefore, must quickly identify those who do not, or will not, have what it takes.

There is another, much smaller, percentage of officer candidates, however, who are not intimidated by the rigors of OCS and who, as a group, have a very low dropout rate. These are the "Mustangs," noncoms who work their way up through the ranks to become officers. Already Marines, they have gone through boot camp and have spent at least a few years in the culture that must seem so hostile and foreign to most college grads. This is not to say that they do not hustle when their OCS drill instructor shouts out commands; they jump just as fast as their collegiate counterparts. But, surely, they have a great psychological advantage by knowing the rules of the game, having played it before.

Not only does the NCO officer candidate have a greater comfort level with the training than his counterparts; the Marine Corps has a greater comfort level with him. After all, he has already proven himself once; chances are he'll do it again at officer training. He is also a Marine who wants to stay a Marine, not a college kid who thinks he wants to be a Marine officer.

In the business world, we frequently hear the term *new blood*. New blood is supposed to infuse new ideas and new energy into a company made lethargic with "old blood." And certainly, bringing in new people from various backgrounds is necessary to prevent the kind of corporate inbreeding that has made some major companies slow to adapt to today's dynamic market. No manager in search of additional personnel wants to be restricted to interviewing only existing employees.

But developing managers out of existing employees has its advantages. The individual is not being hired on the basis of a slick resume and highly developed interviewing skills. He or she is a known—and a proven—entity. The applicant has announced his ambition by applying for a managerial position and can back up his qualifications with a work ethic witnessed by all in his department. The decision to accept or deny the application of an existing employee is based on a body of evidence, not the "hunch" that follows an interview with a complete stranger.

Promoting from within also has a positive impact on the existing workforce, which sees that it is possible to move up the ladder within the organization. Hiring from without often gives the reverse impression. The new manager from the ranks usually has immediate credibility with the current workforce, which trusts in his years on the job. While there are risks associated with promoting from within (e.g., the other employees may have considered him a sycophant; he knows the answers you want to hear), they are minimized if you have a stringent, objective interviewing process and uncompromised qualifications for the position.

Lead by Example

The Hollywood conception of a Marine Corps sergeant is such a universal cliché that it may come as a shock to learn that all Marine NCOs do not get in the faces of their men and bark out orders through a clenched cigar. Even in boot camp, where there is a lot of necessary intimidation, the drill instructors finish training more as mentors than monsters. Certainly, out of boot camp, the Marine NCO does not have to resort to intimidation. That kind of leadership, as the commandant has said, "goes only as far as the arm can reach." As soon as the dictatorial sergeant is out of sight, his influence vanishes as well.

The authority of the Marine NCO does not rest on fear; its foundation is the well-earned respect of equally tough men. He leads, and inspires, by being the man he wants his troops to become.

The NCO personifies his expectations of the men he commands. He wants his Marines to look "squared away" and so dresses and marches smartly himself. Since he wants to instill instant obedience, his men will see him obey instantly when an officer commands. He wants his men to be aggressive in combat, so he himself is the epitome of aggressiveness. The Marine Corps NCO, through his own behavior, creates a desire to be like him.

In the corporation, can it always be said that management leads by example? To the degree that it can be said, the company will be blessed with a dynamic workforce. But, in today's lower-level corporate culture of wages and rights, the savvy employee who won't go an extra inch, not to mention the extra mile, without the obligatory overtime is difficult enough to motivate. If the supervisor is less than a role model, the task is impossible. The inspired employee, however, will go beyond himself without reward. This characteristic should not be exploited; it should be cultivated. And workers who perform to a higher standard should be rewarded. But it is amazing how many managers fail to motivate by their own example.

What Motivates the NCO?

Once we have seen some of the ways in which the NCO motivates his people, the question inevitably arises, "What motivates the NCO?" It certainly can't be the money; every NCO could earn more "on the outside." It isn't the social status; in peacetime the popular culture is indifferent to the military (and not always supportive in war; consider Vietnam). As corny as it sounds, most NCOs are motivated by their love of the Marine Corps, and a corresponding reluctance to sully its record. During their hitch in the Maine Corps, the authors re-peatedly heard their D.I.s and NCOs exclaim, "This is my Ma-rine Corps. I love my Marine Corps." And it's not as if the service is particularly kind to them. A career in the Corps can be a very difficult life, and hard on a marriage. Nonetheless, the loyalty of the NCO borders on the cultic.

How often in the business world do we hear a staff level employee say, "This is my company—I love my company?" If he did say it, he would be ridiculed by his associates or coun-seled by the local union representative. The reader may be as-sured that nobody laughs at a Marine Corps NCO when he says, "This is my Marine Corps."

While it is true that many individuals love working for their respective companies, few will confess to it. Manage-ment does not expect the love of its employees and is uncer-tain how to react to it when encountered. But it is not impossible to elicit strong emotional loyalty from the work-force. Simple gestures such as acknowledging birthdays and congratulating employees on getting married or having a baby go a long way toward engendering reciprocity. The employee who feels cared about will, in turn, care for the company. In-ternal newsletters with a personal emphasis and company-sponsored picnics, golf tournaments, or fishing trips will yield returns of good will out of all proportion to the investment. Scholarship assistance, company stock splits, and matching-funds savings plans all help make an employee feel fortunate to be working for the company. The corporation that shows a genuine interest in the lives of its people will have less turn-over, fewer sick days, and more employees inclined to go "the extra mile."

The Fire-Breathing Dragon—and Nanny

Time after time, when asked what motivated them to advance against the enemy, American soldiers have replied, "I was more afraid of my sergeant." The Hollywood image of a rough-and-ready "sarge" with a cigar butt clamped between his teeth, pushing his troops into a hail of bullets, is not without foundation. NCOs must occasionally motivate with their boots. There are, it must be said, very few occasions that require physical intimidation within the Marine Corps, since recruits are trained from Day One to obey orders. But certainly a ferocious aspect in combat and in training seems to characterize many a Marine NCO.

On the other hand, the NCO is also famous for the nearly maternal care he takes of his troops. After a long day of training, it is he who makes the rounds, making sure everyone is asleep. If a soldier has a personal problem, the first person he usually goes to is his "sarge." The sergeant will defend the reputation of his platoon against all criticism from other NCOs (each of whom quite naturally thinks that his platoon is the best). Like a nagging parent, he will hound his men to take educational correspondence courses offered by the Marines. He will chew out a private for a mistake, then pat him on the back for a job well done. In the same day he may show him the proper way to throw a grenade and to tie a necktie. The NCO is for many teenage recruits the father they never had.

Corporate managers can be fire-breathing dragons, too, if only in terms of their own enthusiasm for a project. Enthusiasm is contagious. There is something in the most cynical nature that wants to lend a hand during times of excitement. Often, simply looking a person in the eye and asking for help is a great motivator. It is surprisingly difficult to refuse a vigorous, earnest request. Knowing that one is being counted on spurs action.

The nanny part comes into play in any number of ways, all cost effective. A good supervisor repays his people for helping him, by helping them. Whenever possible, a manager can interpret company policy to the benefit of the employees. During a special project, he or she can bring in pizza, or call an impromptu unofficial break, or allow those working after hours to come in an hour late the following morning. Certificates, plaques, pins can be awarded with ceremony, involving many in the workforce instead of a single employee of the month. The supervisor can take one of his subordinates to lunch once a month, publicly and without favoritism, so that all know they will have their chance to talk to the boss.

Through a combination of being a fire-breathing dragon and a mentor, the supervisor can enjoy the great leadership success of the Marine Corps' noncommissioned officer.

Be a "Hands-Off" Manager

We have all seen Hollywood variations on the theme of the officer-sergeant relationship. In comedies, the officer is blithely unaware of the wheeling and dealing of his savvy NCO, who manipulates officers and men alike as a kind of underground base commander. The officer may well be aware of an impropriety, but he allows his sergeant to fabricate an explanation. We also have all seen movies in which an officer chances upon a fistfight between two soldiers. He demands to know what has been going on; and his sergeant assures him that the men were practicing self-defense together. The officer stares hard at the offenders, who nod in agreement with their sergeant. He then stares hard at the sergeant, who is the portrait of innocence. The officer accepts his sergeant's explanation, suggests that the men have had enough "self-defense" practice, and walks off.

These are Hollywood fictions, of course (a Marine Corps officer would never tolerate any behavior that might threaten unit cohesiveness), but they do illustrate, to the point of caricature, the officer's dependence upon his NCO to handle the daily activities of military life. Resolving issues before they are escalated up the chain of command is the job of the NCO. The sergeant is expected to take care of such matters and receives a sharp glance from his officer should he be confronted with a matter that could have been resolved at a much lower level. The Marine NCO deals with the day-to-day problems within his world with all the aplomb of a liaison between upper management and the rank and file—which is exactly what he is. Most officers freely attribute their successful careers to their own NCOs, who ran interference for them so that they could, in turn, run interference for their own commanding officers.

This is not to suggest that an officer does not want to be bothered with news from the rank and file. He is, in fact, keenly interested in the well-being of his men. He does not turn away from troubling issues; he can't afford to—the officer is responsible for whatever happens in his command. And he never wants to be blindsided by something his sergeant tried to sweep under the rug. But, it is safe to say that the Marine Corps officer delegates a great deal of the running of a platoon, company, or battalion to a trusted NCO.

In the business world, we often hear someone praised for being a "hands-on manager." And at first glance, it may seem that being intimately involved with all aspects of running a business is a very praiseworthy characteristic. But there is a downside to being a hands-on manager.

Managers who are obsessively immersed in every detail of every operation greatly overestimate their own abilities to administer, while underestimating the abilities of their subordinates, who were hired to get the job done. After all, why were they hired if they aren't needed? The truth is, the manager does need them, and his intrusion into their sphere of responsibility gives the perception of a lack of confidence.

Hands-on managers unknowingly pull the rug out from under their subordinate managers in other ways. Employees will look to them to override punitive decisions made by their immediate supervisors. If these decisions are overturned, or if there is even the perception that they may be overturned, the hands-on manager will find himself besieged by employees appealing for his intervention.

Hands-on managers, of course, cannot do literally everything; they still must delegate some tasks to others. Unfortunately, the things these kinds of managers consider too trivial for their involvement really *are* trivial. Subordinate managers find themselves demeaned, responsible for operations that offer nothing in the way of opportunities for advancement or for increased professional capacity. Seeing no future in working for a company run by a one-man gang, they leave. Even if they stay, their growth has been stunted. The hands-on manager, depending upon his level within the organization, inadvertently threatens the survival of his department, or the entire company, by not preparing his subordinates to take the lead when he is no longer there. He would have better served his company had he let those closest to the task take responsibility for it. After all, that is what the whole rank and structure of the chain of command has been designed for—in the Marines and in business.

Discourage Excessive Unit Identification

In the U.S. Army, there seems to be a shoulder patch for every conceivable unit, from paratroop divisions to the base marching band. Colorful, imaginative, these uniform "tattoos" are so numerous and in such variety that they have become the passion of collectors. They are worn proudly by the soldiers, who are pleased to be publicly identified as belonging to such famous divisions as the 82nd Airborne, the First Armored, or the Green Berets. The navy, too, has special uniforms, insignias, and patches reserved for submariners, underwater demolition teams (a.k.a. "frogmen"), SEALS, and Naval Air.

Things are different in the Marine Corps. Gunnery Sergeant Brian Swanson, MCRD San Diego, is an accredited combat water survival instructor, having had to undergo a rigorous three-week training course in the ocean waters off San Diego and Hawaii. He is one of the handful of exceptionally fit individuals to have completed the psychologically and physically demanding course, which includes swimming a total of thirty-seven miles. Yet, to look at him in uniform, one would never know of his specialty.

"We don't believe in patches or berets," he explains. "We're all Marines here, and we're all good at different things. The main thing is, we're all Marines, and it doesn't get any better."

This lack of emphasis on unit identity prevents the elitist

subcultures that have formed in the other branches of the military. The Green Berets are proud to distinguish themselves from the average army soldier; air force bomber and fighter pilots hardly talk to each other and pursue separate career paths; and submariners live in a secret service all their own. Marines are certainly proud to be different as well—from the other services, but not from each other. Unit identity is not necessary within an organization that believes that nothing exceeds being a Marine.

In every workplace, there are cliques. People tend to aggregate on the basis of department, seniority, or ethnicity and form little subcultures of their own. They eat together in the lunchroom, take coffee breaks together, and watch the developments within the company from a group perspective. Cliques can cause resentment among employees who do not belong to the "in crowd" and who, in self-defense, form cliques of their own.

Cliques are a fact of life and should not be combated. It is management's goal not to break up friendships but to help build new ones. It must expand the comfort zone of its employees and encourage new associations. At company outings, such as the annual picnic, a professional organizer can get away with a lot more than a fellow employee trying to get everybody to mingle. For example, the organizer can set up a softball game with great hoopla and then break up the teams so that an employee finds himself playing first base for the "other" team. Soon he will find himself rooting for his new buddies. At the workplace, management can institute a "rotating chairs" day in the lunchroom so that people are encouraged to eat lunch with those outside the usual group.

A buddy-system can be set up for certain company functions, like taking inventory, joining individuals from opposite ends of the company, who now must spend the day together performing a serious function. Mentor-systems can be introduced, giving new employees the benefit of a more experienced employee's guidance and, one hopes, friendship.

Management must always talk in company-wide terms,

treating administration, sales, production, service, and other functions equally. Each employee should feel he or she is in the right department for advancement. If a big order comes in, management might hold a special lunch (it doesn't matter if it's catered or pot-luck) for the entire company and make it clear during the announcement how each and every department played an integral part in this success. An internal newsletter should be distributed, lauding the contributions of individuals toward the collective company-wide goal. Bumper stickers and T-shirts promoting a unified mission should abound. At every opportunity management must emphasize the big picture. Just as every Marine Corps combat action is an integrated effort of air, ground, and sea forces, every corporate success is a consequence of many departments all pulling in the same direction.

Institutionalize the Supervisor as Teacher

In the Marine Corps, young aspiring officers are taught, for the most part, by sergeants. For months, sergeants, not officer instructors, are commanding the very men they will soon obey. These NCO instructors are as hard on the officer candidates, if not more so, as on the enlisted men in boot camp. For both groups, the NCO is feared, respected, obeyed, and admired as the teacher of how to stay alive on the battlefield.

The Marine Corps has chosen to exalt the NCO because he personifies the heart and soul of the Corps. He knows how the Marine Corps works better than any other rank and is the perfect individual to hand down the hard lessons of war, learned over the generations. In their respective basic training camps, both the private and the aspiring officer look to the NCO for instruction, for leadership, and for approval. Boot camp leaves such an indelible stamp on the subconscious of anyone who has gone through it that the search for approval from the Marine NCO never really leaves one, even if he becomes a general. Many an officer will snap out an order to his troops with impressive authority, then glance sideways to read the reaction on his sergeant's face.

It is ironic that in the military, which has more of a social caste system than the comparatively democratic modern corporation, there is actually a greater respect for the lower-level managers (the NCOs) from upper management (the officers). Even though the officers, NCOs, and privates all go to their respective clubs and socialize within their own groups, there is a flow of influence from one stratum to another. Corporations go out of their way to create a culture of equality, but, for all the openness, there is much less synergy between upper and lower-level management.

Companies would do well to emulate the Marine Corps and institutionalize lower-level managers as the teachers. MBAs fresh out of college may feel they have little to learn from a factory floor supervisor, but nobody knows better the day-to-day procedures of their departments and the impact company policies have on the rank and file. The upper-level manager who is taught by the corporate equivalent of the NCO benefits in many ways. He learns how the company works from a unique vantage point, making friends "in the ranks" and learning whom to call for help. He learns what will motivate and inspire the department and, at the same time, what orders would be reasonable. He impresses production with his eagerness to learn and his willingness to get his hands dirty.

Identify Your Good "Followers"

Because every Marine, regardless of rank, is carrying out somebody's orders, leadership is a curious mixture of assertiveness and doing what one is told. "Before you can lead, you've got to learn how to follow," explains First Sergeant Richard A. Hawkins, Director of the Staff NCO Academy at Marine Corps Base, Hawaii. "It may sound crazy, but a good follower will be a good leader."

From the moment the recruit gets off the bus at boot camp, leaving the friendly world of civilian life behind, he or she is subjected to countless orders, beginning with the trivial and eventually ending up in the realm of life and death decisions. The popular image of instant obedience is true. Every Marine immediately accepts an order but then goes about trying to find a way to carry it out—a process that, depending upon the directive, can require great initiative. An order does not tell one *how* to do it—just to "do it."

So, when a Marine "follows" orders, he is simultaneously problem solving. "Following" is not a matter of blind obedience; the eyes are wide open, assessing the situation and looking for solutions. A good "follower"—one who cheerfully accepts orders and does not shy away from opportunities to overcome obstacles—by definition makes a good leader.

In today's business world, where strong personalities achieve notoriety by "thinking out of the box" and winning bold gambles, no one wants to describe himself, or herself, as a "good follower." The connotation is that of an unimaginative plodder, who keeps his head down until the job eventually gets done, almost of its own accord. There are a great many young General Custers today who impatiently rush past the corporate soldier on a personal, not a collective, quest for glory.

But good "followership" is an important discipline that must not be minimized by media images of charismatic, "take-charge" leaders. The corporate soldier who steadily pursues his or her mission, circumventing obstacles with imagination and initiative, all the way to its conclusion—leaving nothing undone, even the unglamorous details—is a leader in the making. (It is interesting to note that the vast majority of decorated Marine heroes make disappointing interviews; the newsmen are confounded by their nonflamboyant bearing and their eagerness to give the real credit to the men they served with.)

Because future leaders usually do not open the lobby doors and announce themselves as such, management must learn to recognize the leadership potential within its employees. The larger the organization, the more difficult this task may be and the more proactive management must become.

A simple way to separate those willing to step up and accept new challenges from those who shy away from personal risk is to ask for volunteers. The employee who willingly agrees to shoulder more responsibilities, especially when his or her additional efforts are not associated with reward (almost anybody will volunteer for "overtime"), is likely to have the company mission at heart. As important as the "ready attitude," is the capacity to good-naturedly handle the additional workload, without martyrdom and without expectations of great praise.

Volunteerism outside the company is important, as well. Managers should pay particular attention to the resumes that highlight affiliations outside the workplace. Does the employee belong to a service organization, such as Rotary or Lions, or to a self-improvement club like Toastmasters? Is he or she an officer in the organization, making use of administrative skills easily applied to the job? Does the person participate in sports or coach a team? All of these extra curricular activities demonstrate energy, initiative, and leadership potential.

Management should pay attention to those toward whom the other employees seem to gravitate. Who is often elected to be group spokesperson? Whose suggestions are readily accepted by the rank and file as unofficial orders? Which individuals look like leaders, in terms of bearing and physical poise under pressure? Who stays late or comes in early? Who readily admits to mistakes, even though you, as manager, have no way of knowing that a mistake was even made? Who is a team player or, even better, a natural team leader? And who follows through with every assignment, leaving nothing undone?

Conversely, management must keep a sharp eye for negative, often "off-the-record" behavior that indicates the truer character of the employee. Does he or she joke about cheating on income tax? Which employees have no qualms about using the company fax or postage meter for personal use, believing the "company can afford it"? Whose expense reports chronically give you an uneasy feeling, even though there is nothing of major significance to question? Which individuals seem incapable of going against the group, valuing unqualified friendship over personal moral certainty?

Foster a "No Secrets Culture"

In any organization in which individuals contend for a limited number of promotions, it is a temptation to play one's cards close to the vest. The little secrets of success, acquired over years on the job, are not generally shared with rival employees. We tend to think of the tricks of the trade as our own personal property (forgetting those who may have shared with us) and see no need to qualify others for the promotion we covet. And, while the withholding of knowledge may profit us on the climb up the ladder of success, the organization suffers.

The Marine Corps does not tolerate proprietary secrets between its members. Knowledge must be shared, for the very simple reason that individuals die in combat and their fellow Marines must take over with every advantage the original possessed. The success of the Corps itself is more important than that of a particular Marine. It would be unthinkable for a Marine to jeopardize the proficiency of his unit in order to embellish his own career.

This is not to suggest that the individual Marine is without ambition. A military career is much more competitive than one in private enterprise, especially in these days of downsizing. Every Marine does his or her best and hopes to be recognized for it. Certainly, part of the pleasure of carrying out a mission is the "well done" received at its completion. But, as difficult as it may be for an outsider to appreciate, the love of the organization itself prompts most Marines to do what is right for the Corps, even at personal expense. One has only to read the combat medal citations to see how far the commitment to mission can lead certain individuals. Phrases like "at great personal risk," "without regard for one's own safety," and "the ultimate sacrifice" describe the heroic measures taken by individual Marines who thought of nothing but the collective goal.

How can the company create a "no-secrets" environment in which images of personal success come almost as an afterthought to getting the job done? For one thing, the success of every manager must be judged on the basis of the success of his or her own people. Staff Sergeant John LaMantia explains how it works in the Marine Corps: "My success is based upon how successful the men I supervise are. If my guys aren't promoted when they're eligible, you'd better believe I get the phone calls. My C.O. wants to know what I'm doing wrong."

Companies must make it clear that every associate, not just management, is evaluated upon and rewarded for his or her contributions to the team effort. It seems as if every other business on the block has an Employee of the Month program, which is usually based on individual achievement. Why not begin a Team Player of the Month award, based on individual sacrifice? When individuals are awarded, and rewarded, for giving selflessly of their time and knowledge toward the common good, the behavior may become a bit less selfless, but certainly more abundant.

Just as the National Basketball Association keeps statistics of "assists" (i.e., the practice of passing the ball off to a teammate who is in better scoring position, even though you might have scored the basket yourself), managers must keep a running tab of workplace "assists" and compensate accordingly. Imagine the impact upon a department if the next promotion were to be given not to the top producer but to the top "teamplayer." Soon, people would be falling all over themselves to contribute (perhaps a little ostentatiously) toward the common good. The entire workforce can be rewarded, too, in profit-sharing programs or "one-time" rewards such as a new employee recreation room or perhaps a company promise to pay everybody's medical deductible for the year.

In an effort to promote a "no-secrets" company culture, Diebold, the leading automated teller machine (ATM) manufacturer in the nation, publishes an internal, not-for-distribution Spotlight On Success newsletter, in which employees are interviewed when they have a "personal" success. Invariably, the achievement is revealed to be a collective one—not to diminish the individual's efforts, but to highlight all who were involved. The newsletter has a threefold impact: (1) the team responsible for a significant order is recognized and praised; (2) other associates learn from reading the interview how this feat was accomplished and can emulate it themselves; and (3) the self-esteem of all employees of the company goes up a notch when they read the news of the resulting big order.

Implement a Manager's School

For more than two hundred years, the preparation for being a noncommissioned officer could best be characterized as "on the job training." The legendary performance of generations of Marine Corps NCOs would suggest that this informal procedure served the nation rather well. In 1971, however, the Marine Corps decided the system could be improved. "Sergeant's School" was born, offering a curriculum that would benefit all NCOs. Formal courses in leadership, training management, personnel administration, war-fighting tactics, and military justice are today taught to every sergeant within months of his promotion. Sergeant's School ensures that every NCO, regardless of his particular "on-the-job training" experiences, learns the identical leadership principles that the Marine Corps wants to pass on.

Today, the Marine Corps sergeant is a well-trained professional, "on the same page" as his peers, skilled in war-fighting tactics and personnel management. This is not to say he has lost the flair that distinguishes him from his counterpart in the other services. The rough-and-ready sergeant of the "Old Corps" would no doubt approve of his modern replacement. Today's Marine sergeant is just as colorful and just as tough as his predecessor, but better trained at his job. The Marine Corps no longer takes it for granted that experience alone makes a good leader.

Companies would do well to recognize that years on the job do not necessarily make a good manager. By creating a Manager's School, the company can ensure that the desired leadership principles are institutionalized across the board. Upper management can rest assured that its management directives will be understood and practiced by each and every leader. A formal school also impresses upon the newly appointed manager that he has crossed a point of no return in his professional life. No longer an "eight-to-five" employee, he will voluntarily submit to an ongoing process of constant improvement.

Instead, he will belong to a new peer group, each member sharing a similar burden, each committed to a new life within the organization. The smiles may be less frequent, but will convey deeper satisfaction when they come. All managers, regardless of department, will be pulling in the same direction, trained in the same crucible, committed to the identical personal and collective goals. Each will be conditioned to avoid the temptation of single-handedly performing the tasks he or she used to do so well. Leaders themselves, they will cultivate the leadership qualities of their subordinates by allowing them to take charge.

Support Ongoing Education

At every step up the promotional path, the career NCO is encouraged to take Professional Military Education courses, which have been designed for the responsibilities of each rank and which cover material from war-fighting skills to counseling to military law. A correspondence portion is followed by a resident program, which can take up to six weeks. These courses are extremely demanding, mentally and physically (there are several grueling physical fitness tests during the course), and they are purely voluntary. Those who choose not to participate have effectively taken themselves out of the running for promotion, however.

One would think that the PME instructors, NCOs themselves, would have a fairly relaxed attitude toward their fellow veteran Marines. But many an experienced sergeant has sweated bullets completing the courses. No quarter is given for experience; these NCOs have to be as earnest as they were in boot camp. Those who take the PME must excel in it. Class standings are entered into the personnel files of each student and become a very strong criterion for the next promotion. The end result of the PME program is an exceedingly professional core of career noncommissioned officers, each trained at every level of increased responsibilities.

A company that wishes to create a similar foundation for success would do well to urge, or even require, participation in ongoing education or certification classes by its employees. Just as professional organizations mandate that doctors, accountants, and real estate agents take a minimum of forty hours of approved continuing education classes every year at the risk of having their licenses suspended for failure to comply, companies in free enterprise are entitled to expect their associates to continue to improve upon themselves. Job ads in the classified sections of the newspaper are quite specific about mandatory educational requirements; it should come as no surprise to the newly hired employee that he cannot simply rest on his laurels. Pay raises and promotions are frequently linked with educational achievements; schoolteachers, for example, are awarded additional income in almost direct proportion to their possession of advanced degrees.

The company, of course, should take an active role in either providing the continuing education itself or reimbursing the cost of outside alternatives, such as courses offered by accredited colleges, private schools, trade associations, and professional training organizations like the American Management Association. The important point is that employees should never look upon these courses as formalities to be suffered through because of management's obsession for self-improvement. Like the Marine NCOs, they must feel the pressure to perform, regardless of their tenure or ranking within the organization.

Lifeboat Leadership

Leadership cultivation begins from Day One of basic training—actually before that, unofficially, during the recruitment
"pool" program—and continues throughout a Marine's career.
As soon as practical, Marines are assigned missions that they
are expected to carry out on their own initiative. The person
giving the order, however, makes it clear that he or she is there
as a resource.

"I tell my officers and NCOs," says Colonel Richard Dallaire, assistant chief of staff, Quality Management Department,
at Marine Corps Recruit Depot, San Diego "Here is your mission; go and accomplish it, but come to me if you have questions. I always want my personnel to know that I am here for
them—not to do their jobs for them but to offer advice and
counsel. That's how I learned. That's how every Marine
learns." The Marine Corps does not believe in "sink or swim,"
they believe in teaching how to swim.

NCOs pass this tradition down to their own men. "I call it
'lifeboat leadership,'" says Gunnery Sergeant Paul Washington at MCRD, "I'll give a man an order and expect him to carry
it out on his own. But he knows I'm nearby in the lifeboat, in
case he needs help. So, I'll talk to him, give him some advice,
then throw him back in the water until he gets it right."

Ironically, there are corporate cultures that can be
tougher, or at least less forgiving, than that of the Marine
Corps. There are companies that believe the challenges of
leadership will soon weed out those who are unable to lead.
This "sink-or-swim" philosophy would be abhorrent to most
Marines, who have had the benefit of influential mentors.

The Marine Corps knows that the cultivation of leadership qualities within an individual is an investment of time
and resources that may not immediately bear fruit. Even com-
mandants were stumbling 2nd lieutenants once. Fortunately,
the system allows for personal development, and many a 2nd
lieutenant has matured into a legendary leader.

Business leaders must see through the stumbling "2nd

lieutenant phase" of managerial development. Even if a prospective manager completely fails at a given task, his or her character, honesty, and determination not to let it happen again may be more important. Of course, the chances of failure diminish in proportion to one's preparation for the task. Managers must see to it that their people are fully briefed and trained for what they are expected to accomplish. Do they clearly understand their mission? Do they know what departments and individuals can support them, so time isn't spent reinventing the wheel? Are they comfortable enough to approach you, the boss, for counsel and advice? Do you ask to see their plan so that you know they're on the right track?

Managers at all levels are made, not born. The corporation has the unique opportunity to forge managers in its own image and to perpetuate its mission for generations to come. The "sink-or-swim" school of leadership is incompatible with long term success. Why let events make or break your future standard-bearers? Companies that expect to flourish decades from now must create a culture in which their leaders are taught how to swim.

Move People Up or Out

The culture of the Marine Corps is a brutally honest one, especially in terms of knowing where one stands within the hierarchy of the organization. The NCO's peers can tell at a glance how long he has been in the service and how far he has gotten. The NCO is a walking billboard of personal success, or lack thereof. On his sleeves are the hash marks, each one representing four years of service. On his shoulder are his stripes, signifying the rank he has achieved in that period of time. It does not take a rocket scientist to very quickly determine whether the NCO is a rising star or on his way out of the Corps.

Sometimes, when the numbers of hash marks and the numbers of stripes don't seem to agree, it is because the NCO was "busted," or, reduced in rank. A stripe is taken away, more evidence of the brutally honest system within the Corps.

Instead of being secretly docked in pay, the NCO receives a punishment that is out there for all to see. And all may see the busted NCO's redemption as well, when the stripe is returned to his shoulder.

An NCO is expected to work his way up the chain of command within a reasonable time frame. If he does not, it will become clear to him—and to everybody around him—that he has no future in the Marine Corps. No new job titles are created to salve the ego of a Marine who has been passed over for promotion, as often happens in private enterprise. He either makes the next rank, or he doesn't. Knowing full well that the odds are against him, he can try again the next time he is up for promotion. The second failure means he will be given his walking papers.

So the Marine Corps, which once issued the challenge to the young recruit, "Do you have what it takes to become one of The Few, The Proud?," issues a much less publicized challenge well into his career: "Do you *still* have what it takes?" The pressure to continue to perform is even stronger in the modern day, downsized Corps. The public conception of burned-out military men hanging onto their jobs just to "get in my twenty" years for retirement has no foundation in the Marine Corps, which has created a culture of upward mobility or bust.

What makes such a culture possible is the clarity of the career path. There is no such thing as a lateral move within the Marine Corps; each individual moves up, or he moves out. The Corps is left with an organization populated with successful, aggressive Marines bent on performing at their best. In the business world, however, the career path is not usually a straight vertical line; it is more like a family tree, with branches spreading laterally into hastily created and sometimes inexplicable job titles.

In many companies there is no sense of collective momentum up the promotional ladder. There is, in fact, sometimes quite the opposite. Managers point with pride to employees who have sat at the same desk for twenty years, as if they were living testimonials to the benevolent nature of the workplace. While seniority can certainly be a good thing, one's years with the company should be a quest, not a sentence. The employee who is encouraged and required to move up in the ranks—or to take on additional responsibilities in his current position— will be the beneficiary of a policy that requires all associates to keep pace with the strides of the organization. He would be proficient at many tasks and would not be heard crying, should he be laid off, "I don't know how to do anything else!"

It is not cold and heartless to expect one's employees to constantly improve themselves. The employment contract is not unconditional; there are a number of "pre-nuptials" on both sides. Nor is it heartless to discharge those who cannot or will not keep pace with the strides of the corporation. Economic life itself encourages the survival of the fittest; to suggest that a business should somehow be a refuge from the competition of the marketplace is ridiculous and suicidal. No company can survive by attempting to become a home for its employees. Like the Marine Corps, it must create a brutally honest environment where all are expected to grow in professional capacity—or stagnate somewhere else.

Institute Annual Subject Readiness Tests

Behind all Marine Corps policy is the Corps' single-minded dedication to combat readiness. For this reason, all NCOs and officers, no matter how proficient at their jobs, must pass a semiannual physical fitness test. Failure to pass is considered very serious and can, if not corrected, be career ending. In today's downsized Corps, the overweight Marine—or even one who doesn't look good in his uniform—is literally an endangered species. One has only to visit a Marine base to see how seriously the fitness tests are taken; it would be a safe bet that no out-of-shape Marines could be found.

Physical fitness, while clearly desirable, is not a mission critical attribute of the corporate soldier. But a total familiarity with one's professional environment is certainly critical to individual and collective success. A company will never prevail in the competitive marketplace unless its associates are exceptionally competent in their fields. Just as the Marine Corps applies the iron law of physical fitness to all Marines, regardless of their performance of their duties, the forward-thinking company should require all of its associates to take annual "subject readiness" examinations.

These tests should measure an individual's knowledge of his specific responsibilities, as well as of the trends and recent developments within his general field. For example, an accountant in Accounts Payable should be required to have a grasp of the principles and procedures of Accounts Receivable and of the software developments within these highly specialized disciplines. Salespeople should be tested not only on the products they represent but also on the equivalent products offered by the competition, as well as on the trends within the industry.

Each and every employee should dread these examinations, which in reality need not be all that difficult, so long as the associate is motivated to read more and to think more about the future of his or her own field. But the scores should be taken seriously, entered into the personnel file, and referred to during performance reviews.

The effect of annual subject readiness tests on some corporate cultures would be nothing short of catastrophic. Many a thirty-year company drone would shake in his boots at the prospect of taking such a test and of suddenly being required to meet objective standards. The salesperson who hasn't had to stir a brain cell once he got his "spiel" down would find himself compelled to learn more about his own product and those of his competition. Every associate, fearing the test would expose his individual weaknesses, would go out and fill in the gaps in their knowledge before examination day. Just as the thought of a semiannual physical fitness test causes most Marines to push away from the dinner table, an annual subject readiness test would stir many an employee out of his or her comfort zones and into the dynamic regions of the worker's chosen field. Everybody would benefit, with the exception of the indolent, who would leave this demanding corporate culture and end up on the payroll of the competition.

Instill a Spirit of Competition

Competition pervades boot camp. Virtually every activity, with the possible exception of going to the bathroom, is a competitive event. Recruits generally compete in groups, such as a three-man fire team, twelve-man squad, and so on. Even trivial assignments such as picking up cigarette butts off "the grass" (Marine-speak for any surface other than the parade black top), or watering the "uprights" (trees) become serious contests between the units involved. Pennants for the winners of more warlike events, such as pugil stick fighting and shooting on the rifle range, are as coveted as sacred relics and flown before the platoon during the public graduation ceremony.

Of course, most young men and women are not strangers to competition. Indeed, many school and parent groups have complained that growing up in America is too competitive and that our children are overexposed to the stress of competition—from Little League and Peewee football to the only slightly more intense rivalries of school. Friendships are often impossible between teenagers simply because they attend antagonistic schools.

What makes the rivalries fostered in Marine Corps boot camp so different? All the competition is in the family. Every recruit is struggling toward the same goal—graduation as a full-fledged Marine—and all who make it are winners. There isn't one prize, but 40,000 "prizes" every year. Every graduate shares the bond of common experience (in this case, "uncommon" experience). On graduation day, each basks in the glow of the other. And, conversely, before graduation day, every Marine takes just as much "guff" as the other, even those who are in the honor platoon.

The competition between Marines does not stop there. Throughout his career, a Marine will join forces with his unit and strive against another platoon or company of his brothers—in military exercises and maneuvers. The competition, being between warriors who already consider themselves the best, has a kind of "pro bowl" quality to it that the other services, frankly, sometimes find irritating. But the competition never stops.

Of course, many corporations today promote contests between factory shifts, administrative departments, and sales personnel. But how clear are the goals to management? The Marine Corps couldn't care less which platoon wins which event; it is trying to foster teamwork and self-confidence among each and every recruit and Marine. The great achievement of the intense competition within boot camp is that everybody feels like a winner. And this experience is not easily duplicated.

The corporation can begin to emulate this process by fostering many contests. If the goal is to promote teamwork, the "how to" of the competition can be left up to the initiative of the teams involved. A production goal can be set, for example, calling for a 10 percent increase, the only rules being that safety and quality cannot be sacrificed and that overtime is not to be part of the solution. Whatever the outcome, the rewards must be rapid and proportionate. Management may very well see that some of the practices recently developed by the teams make sense for the long term.

One of the things a business can do to create a universal feeling of winning is to create a handicap system in its competitions. In a sales contest, for example, it is not fair to pit a relative newcomer, who may have just mastered the product, against an experienced veteran with established accounts. The goal, after all, is to create self-confidence in the one and to maintain it in the other. Both should have an equal opportunity to bonus.

Businesses must also remember that even modest, trivial contests, such as seeing which department can make the fewest long-distance phone calls or which can make the most efficient use of the office supplies, can be worthwhile. After all, the river of waste within most organizations is fed by numerous tiny streams. Even the old-fashioned contests such as monitoring attendance or rewarding the unit with the fewest accidents, can still create an enthusiastic response, especially if rewarded by an early afternoon off at the end of the month.

Formalize the Grievance Procedure

A major source of discontentment in the workplace is the lack of a formal policy on how to resolve grievances. Often, an employee who is never offered an opportunity to let off steam internalizes his dissatisfaction until he can no longer contain it. He may resign in exasperation—or worse. A Marine, on the other hand, knows that he can always have the ear of his superiors, to the top of the chain of command if need be. The process is called Requesting Mast and is available to every Marine. It is a serious request, and is taken seriously by all the intermediaries up the line, who try to resolve the issue before it reaches the commanding general's desk. Indeed, most grievances are resolved at a lower level. But, if not mollified, a Marine knows he can take his case all the way to the top—at which point he may or may not get satisfaction. Either way, he is protected by a procedure that no superior, NCO, or officer can interrupt.

Management should consider formalizing a pathway to the top. Most likely, grievances will be settled at a much lower level of management; but, every now and then, somebody will work his way up to the very top, and the word will get around that this is possible. It is very likely that the CEO's decision, like that of an appellate judge's, will reaffirm the original, but the employee may feel somewhat vindicated in terms of the procedure he was able to force. He has been taken seriously by his company, so much so that the chief executive officer has had to listen to his problem. Having exhausted all possible avenues—and having been allowed to—the chances are very good that he has exhausted his energy on the issue, as well. Most people who walk out of a courtroom after their case has been lost accept the decision because, at the very least, they've "had their day in court."

Needless to say, if a grievance procedure is to have any credibility with the rank and file of the company, there can be no retaliation by management. Once the issue has been dealt with, it must be forgotten. The various steps up the ladder of appeal must also be prompt. The whole idea of a grievance procedure is to empower the employee; nothing could make him feel more helpless than having his case put on indefinite hold by a Kafkaesque bureaucracy. For his part, the employee must be made to realize—by its very formality—that this procedure is not to be taken lightly or used for unsubstantiated complaints.

Reach Out to the Families of the Rank and File

It may come as a surprise to learn that even a "blood and guts" company commander will stop in the middle of a busy day to accept a call from the spouse of one of his Marines. The Marine Corps, for all its tough, masculine traditions, is extremely solicitous of the "other half" of the Corps—the families of its members. Many a commanding officer has stubbed out his cigar and jumped to his feet at the entrance of a Marine wife with a problem.

It wasn't always that way. The attitude of the "Old Corps" toward marriage and family could be summed up in the famous statement, "If the Marine Corps wanted you to have a wife, they would have issued you one." The life of a Marine was hard back then, as it is today, with long absences from home; but today, it is not made more difficult by an indifferent command structure. The modern Corps is, in fact, more proactive in family outreach programs than even the most progressive organization in private enterprise.

A vast network of volunteer Marine wives works in concert with the officers and senior NCOs on any number of programs designed to keep the family strong and healthy and, above all, supportive of their Marines. The Marine Corps knows full well that the day will come when a valuable officer or NCO will have the choice of remaining in the Corps or reentering a civilian lifestyle that is much less demanding on his family. No Marine is going to "re-up" if the spouse is not totally "on board."

One of the ways to encourage this kind of support is to make the wife aware of the importance of her husband's work. Drill instructors, for example, are away from home a great deal. Even though they live only a short distance from base, the D.I. must be with his recruits virtually twenty-four hours a day. It is no accident, therefore, that the only people invited to witness the private and very moving internal graduation ceremony of The Crucible are the wives of the drill instructors. The Marine van stops at the bottom of Grim Reaper; the wives and the commanding officers and generals who accompany them *walk* up the hill, in a symbolic gesture of appreciation for the many miles hiked by the drill instructors and their recruits. There at the top, amid the handclasps and the joyful tears of the graduating recruits, the wives can see for themselves what their absent D.I. husbands have been doing for the past twelve weeks. And they invariably leave the emotional ceremony very proud of their husband's work—the making of Marines.

The life of the corporate soldier can be very demanding, as well, on his or her family. Late hours, stress, business trips, and working weekends can take a heavy toll on the relationships between husbands and wives, parents and children. So often the excuse for not being with one's family is "I have to work." While accurate enough, the phrase may mean very little to a neglected wife or child, who has no clear idea of what "work" entails.

Like the Marine Corps, the corporation must be more solicitous of the "other half" of its workforce—those who must emotionally support the employees. The stereotype of the hard-driving executive who works his way to the top of the ladder at the expense of his family life is both true and false. It is true that many marriages are sacrificed to business careers; but there are very few successful careers that do not enjoy the total support of the individual's family. A manager who is distracted by marital or family problems will not have the emotional foundation for sustained achievement.

The company can do a lot to bring the spouse "on board" by instituting a Family Day, which might include factory tours, new product previews, product demonstrations against the competition, and perhaps a general overview of the year's business. Child day-care programs for single-parent employees, carpool networks, scholarship contributions, and maybe even a company "family counselor" would all make a deep impression on the people you, as an employer, need as allies.

Exalt Seniority

On the forearm sleeve of senior Marines are bold stripes called hash marks, which represent time in service. Each stripe represents four years of experience. Worn proudly, hash marks mean as much as rank to a Marine who has earned them. His peers can tell at a glance that he has "been around" and look naturally to him for guidance. His superiors, too, will expect a bit more from him as a veteran Marine.

Most businesses distribute symbols of seniority, such as lapel pins and wall plaques. But often these tokens are handed over in the manager's office with little or no ceremony. The more fanfare, the more importance the employee will attach to the event. This is not meant to be a cynical suggestion. Every human being—from the mailroom clerk to the chairman of the board of directors—likes to be recognized before his peers for personal achievements. This is why the Corps breaks out the brass band for the awarding of medals and why rough and tough Marines choke back tears of pride as the highest-ranking officer on base personally pins his medal on for him—in front of everybody in the world that matters.

Businesses should exalt seniority—publicly, shamelessly, and with enough fanfare to raise goosebumps on the flesh of the most cynical spectator. And, after the ceremony, there should be some sort of permanent display so that employees passing by are continuously reminded of their own achievements and the achievements of others. National Chemical, for example, honors its senior salespeople by hanging museum-quality portraits in oil, ornately framed, each one lighting up a long hallway like noble ancestors.

Leadership Strategies Checklist

—Standardize the promotional requirements so that all supervisors will have credibility and the respect of the rank and file.
—Create a corporate culture that exalts the workforce.
—Balance management with promotions from within.
—Inspire through personal example.
—Understand that the employee who feels cared for will care about the company.
—Combine fire-breathing enthusiasm with solicitous mentoring.
—Empower those closest to the task to make decisions.
—Expand departmental pride into a corporate-wide phenomenon.
—Institutionalize the supervisor as the corporate teacher.
—Recognize followership as the precursor to leadership.
—Convert personal ambition into commitment to the corporate mission.
—Implement a "manager's school" for all levels of management.
—Require and support continuing education.
—Empower and delegate, but be available to your subordinates.
—Expect all associates to keep pace with the strides of the organization.

—Implement company-wide "subject readiness" tests.
—Promote constructive competition within the organization.
—Provide all associates with a communication path all the way to the top.
—Reach out to the families of the workforce and managerial staff.
—Exalt seniority, while maintaining performance expectations.

4

Middle Management: Leading the Mission

"The relation between officers and enlisted men should in no sense be that of superior and inferior, nor that of master and servant, but rather that of teacher and scholar."

—Major General John A. Lejeune,
13th Commandant, USMC

"I quickly learned that team work—all pulling together toward an identifiable common goal—worked far better than rushing headlong 'over the top' only to discover that no one was behind you."

—Arthur Ochs Sulzberger Sr., Chairman Emeritus,
The New York Times Company,
formerly Captain, USMC

When a son announces that he intends to join the military, the universal parental response (after trying to talk him out of it) is: "Well, at least be an officer; officers have it easier." While officers in every branch of the service are burdened with greater responsibilities, it is true that they are spared much of the drudgery encountered by the enlisted rank and file. The expression "an officer and a gentlemen" sums up the expectations of many college graduates, who look forward to an adventurous military life, without necessarily getting their hands too dirty.

Young people who hope to become Marine Corps officers, however, know full well that they are entering the branch of the armed forces with the most demanding officer training, the highest officer combat casualty rate, and certainly the least amount of comfort in terms of officer amenities. So, right from the start, Marine Corps officer candidates are somewhat unusual individuals, attracted to challenge. Those who are ultimately selected to lead the "nation's finest" then undergo the most profound leadership training on the planet. Managers in private enterprise, who may have trouble enough motivating their own subordinates to work five minutes after the whistle blows, would do well to study these leaders, who inspire their personnel to the extremes of endurance and sacrifice.

Credibility of the Officers

The Marine Corps officer not only commands the respect of his troops; he deserves it. He has endured training more difficult than that of the men he leads. He is as tough physically, if not more so, and well schooled in the strategies that will help his unit succeed in battle. He can walk with assurance in front of the platoon, because he *belongs* there. He is both prepared and entitled to lead, and his men know it.

A manager who has "come up through the ranks" usually does not have a credibility problem (although sometimes he may have an authority problem) with those under his "command." But, because management skills transcend industries, companies often look to the outside for their leaders. Managers new to the company are not immediately credible because they are unknown. Often, employees would more readily accept a new manager if only they knew more about him.

Upper management is often remiss at this time. It is upper management's job to thoroughly introduce every new manager, both in person and in print, to the department he or she will lead. A few days before the official introduction, written "bios" should be distributed by newsletter and company e-mail. This is no time for false modesty, either. The new manager was chosen out of a field of highly qualified candidates; the reasons for the choice should be shared with the organization. Past achievements and current credentials should be trumpeted. Every employee should share upper management's confidence and feel fortunate to have such a leader—who just may take them to higher levels of performance and compensation.

New managers should not be afraid to "show their stuff." There is nothing more confidence inspiring than witnessing the boss deal successfully with a difficult situation. Being a newcomer, the new manager will ask for input from his associates, involving them in the process. When he makes his decision, it should be clear to all that he is quite prepared to personally accept the consequences. Oddly enough, the more a manager tries to shield his department, the more willing his department is to step forward and share his exposure.

Last, every manager must realize deep down inside that he is entitled to lead. Many employees may not appreciate, or even understand, the achievements that qualify one for a management position. But these achievements are legitimate. Education, for example, is not a gift. College degrees and MBA programs are open to all who have the initiative and the drive. Managers should be proud of the achievements that separate them from their subordinates; they have worked hard for the positions they are in, often taking classes and doing "on-the-job" homework into the late hours of the night.

A manager should walk just as tall as a Marine Corps officer in front of his column. Like the officer, he is totally exposed if the collective mission fails and must account alone to upper management. Like the officer, he takes the job home with him and, in a figurative sense, is "the last to sleep and the first to wake." Like the officer, he has the courage to take on responsibilities that would make his subordinates shudder. And, like the Marine Corps officer, he has ambition—a quality not to be sneezed at. Ambition requires several virtues, among them: courage, self-sacrifice, and the ability to delay gratification.

Taking the Same Risks

While young men do not join the Marine Corps because it promises to be a safe way of life, they nonetheless have the reassurance that Marines will never be placed in harm's way recklessly or needlessly. The Marine Corps private and NCO alike have faith that even the most aggressive action will be carefully planned by their commanding officers, who themselves will lead the way. The men know that, whatever the outcome, their officers will share the fate of the platoon.

This sense of trust and commitment would not be possible if the troops knew that their leaders were to be evacuated by helicopter in dire circumstances, leaving them to face the enemy. Just as we, as passengers on a commercial jetliner, are pleased that the pilots do not wear parachutes, Marines take a kind of grim comfort in knowing that their officers will go down with them if the unit is overwhelmed by the enemy.

In business, managers, of course, are very much at risk. If the company's goals are not met, they, not the employees, must sit in the hot seat and account for the department's failure. Ask any manager and he will tell you that managers most certainly share the fate of the other employees within the company—and that they are, in fact, at greater risk, being prepared to take the fall for the poor performance of their subordinates. But, ask any employee, and he will tell you that, when it comes to layoffs, the managers are the last to go.

This conviction is based on a perception, in most cases unfounded, that managers have a higher survival rate because of their association with the top decision makers within the company—relationships the "little guy" could never hope to cultivate. Employees are convinced that, in times of radical downsizing, management will protect itself, at the cost of every working man or woman in the company. Employees also believe managers, due to their access to privileged information, are forewarned of bad weather and able to prepare for the oncoming storm, while the employee is taken by surprise.

So, what can management do, as "pilots" of the company, to show the rest of the passengers that they are not wearing parachutes?

For starters, a manager should publicly associate himself with assigned departmental projects or quotas, staking his own reputation upon the performance of his group. When the department feels that their manager is just as vulnerable as everyone else is, a true team is in the making, one that will go the extra mile for its leader. Conversely, managers who are perceived as immune not only from the struggle to meet expectations but from the consequences of failure can expect nothing "above and beyond the call of duty" from their group.

Managers who desire loyalty must continually give credit to their own people for any and all accomplishments and, like the Marine Corps officer, "take the hit" themselves for the group's failure to meet expectations. Or, as Lieutenant Colonel William Leek, Commanding Officer, Los Angeles Recruiting Station, puts it, "If it's a good job, they did it; if it's a bad job, I did it."

How many sales managers reading this are prepared to take the same risks as their sales force? While most are eager to associate themselves with a sales triumph, many are quick to distance themselves from a failure. Suddenly, the lost opportunity becomes the sole property of the sales rep, who feels abandoned by his superior. Sales managers could change the whole culture of their department by simply putting their own future on the line with their reps. The manager who accompanies his salesperson on the "big calls" and who shares the same fate, win or lose, will gain unprecedented loyalty from his sales force, as well as some valuable street knowledge about the marketplace that will serve him well on the next opportunity.

See the Big Picture

The very nature of Marine Corps warfare demands that the officer have in mind the big picture, the very big picture of an amphibious assault: sea power, jet fighter/bombers, helicopters, tanks, artillery, ground troops, paratroops, and half a dozen other applications of force focused in one vast integrated movement upon an enemy unfortunate enough to resist the Marines. Only the Marine Corps officer, who is charged with carrying out the mission, can truly see the structure behind the chaos of an all-out attack. He is trained, therefore, in every military science brought to bear upon the enemy.

In an age of increasing specialization, the Marine Corps officer stands out as a kind of military Renaissance Man, well versed in the integration of forces at his disposal. He sees the big picture because his very life depends upon seeing the big picture; he and his troops are in the thick of it. One mistake and his unit could become a victim of friendly fire, at the very least.

In civilian life, we often hear the phrase "Jack of all trades, master of none." Dating back to medieval times, it has been a singularly worthless and destructive adage for a thousand years. In today's business environment, with its emphasis upon complexity worship, a "jack of all trades" is precisely what is needed for management. No manager should attempt to master the tasks he must oversee; his greater responsibility to the company is to direct the specialists at his disposal. And that is a very important skill.

Managers who see the big picture of the global marketplace are able to recognize new opportunities for the company or, conversely, current operations that should be divested. Awareness of the big picture helps the manager to (1) see how his own particular department contributes to the overall success of the company, (2) appreciate the contributions of other departments, (3) recognize when a department may be going in the wrong direction, (4) better direct the components of the overall corporate activity that are under his control, and (5) inspire those who report to him by making them aware of their importance to the overall scheme of things.

Ductus Explo (Lead by Example)

Although Marine Corps sergeants take great care to personify the expectations they have of the troops, officers are much more visible and therefore under greater pressure to lead by example. In the daily activities of Marine Corps life, the eyes of his men are always upon him. Marine officers are conscious of this and behave accordingly. An officer who does not want to be humiliated on a cross-country run must be in better shape than his men. Unlike naval officers, who dine separately in the ship's wardroom on (perceived) delicacies, the Marine officer eats the same chow as his men. In fact, whenever hot food is served in the field, he is the last to eat. No Marine officer will put food on his plate until every enlisted man has been served. He is also the last to sleep and the first to awake. In combat, he is the unit's best hope for success and survival on the battlefield. It is no wonder that the enlisted Marine will do anything for his officer.

A manager in private enterprise must, like the Marine Corps officer, remember that the eyes of his people are always upon him. Managers, by virtue of their high visibility, have the opportunity to set the tone of the workplace by personal example. And, good or bad, this example will be noted. A manager who personifies his expectations will be respected. But one who flaunts the double standard by requiring his subordinates to report to work on time and showing up late himself, will only be resented.

Surely most managers attempt to set a positive example. But perhaps their greatest undoing is their own sense of propriety. A manager who is too concerned with appearing "managerial" will give the impression of not being part of the struggle. He will be seen as posing. Marine Corps officers do not pose as leaders; they actively lead their troops through battle or maneuver with an attitude that makes it clear that they consider no task beneath them. Managers who desire the enthusiastic support of their own "troops" should, like the Marine officer, abandon the self-consciousness of command and just get the job done.

Certainly one of the greatest challenges of leading by example is the occasional need to overcome one's own fears. Leading by example can mean doing things that are very uncomfortable, such as going down a deep construction shaft to demonstrate the safety of the elevator to the crew, or even taking part in the talent show at the Christmas party and making a fool of oneself. It often requires great personal courage to be the first to take action, unsure if anybody will follow. Just as a Marine officer never orders his men to do something he wouldn't do, the corporate "officer" must always be prepared to personally show how the task should be done.

Put People Before Paper

The military is famous for an administrative bureaucracy that seems to frustrate even the simplest of desires. There is a form, in triplicate, for every conceivable request; and if a truly novel need arises, a form will be designed for it. Ponderous manuals describe in wearying detail the policies and procedures most soldiers know simply as "red tape." Comedies have been made out of the military's obsession with protocol, in which requisitions for even nonexistent items are rubber-stamped with approval, as long as the proper channels were followed. Exposés have been written, revealing the inefficiencies of the administrative systems in place and the resulting taxpayer shock at the prices paid for the most commonplace items manufactured for the military (two-hundred-dollar toilet seats, one-hundred-dollar screwdrivers).

We're not suggesting that the Marine Corps is without paperwork and red tape, but there is a great sensitivity—from the commandant on down—to taking care of the individual Marine as quickly as possible. "People before paper," says Lieutenant Colonel Ernest Hickson, Operations Officer at Officer Candidate School, Quantico, Virginia. "I've got a ton of paperwork to do; but when I see a Marine standing before my desk, I push it all to the side. The individual Marine always comes first."

The corporate environment is also a very busy place. With the advent of the local area network, the Internet, and a computer on every desk—which was all supposed to reduce administrative time—managers have more to do than ever. It seems as if the more the corporation gives them in the way of available technology, the more they are expected to do with it. Nearly every manager today has a laptop computer and must keep pace with the incessant flow of e-mail on the company's intranet. Hours are spent on the computer generating weekly spreadsheets, reports, and predictions to be sent on to upper management. During the closing hours of every month, managers sequester themselves behind closed doors, under deadline for numerous reports. Pity the employee who knocks on a manager's door during this intense period of electronic "paperwork."

Like the Marine Corps officer, the manager must put his people before his own personal administrative tasks. It may not simply be a matter of pushing the laptop aside upon the entrance of an employee—many will be too timid to seek his help. Today's managers must be proactive, sensitive to the needs of his people. A new employee who must expense a plane ticket to the company training facility before his paychecks kick in may be in need of a cash advance. He probably won't ask for it, but he will certainly be grateful if it is offered by a thoughtful manager. An employee on bereavement leave may need a few more days than the company normally allows; the proactive manager may bend the rules in such a case. If an employee in a company vehicle has an accident, the manager's first words should be "Are you OK? Was anybody hurt?," rather than "Whose fault was it?" or, "How's the car?"

Although willing to grant employee requests, the manager must guard against the appearance of favoritism or the undermining of company policies. If a manager grants additional vacation to one employee, it must be with the proviso that the time will be worked off, after hours, upon return. Otherwise, the favor will become a benefit, expected by all under his authority. If an employee has failed to complete his own paperwork, such as failing to get a field authorization signed or submitting an expense without the receipt, the manager must make it clear that this one "break" is the exception and that company policies must be followed to the letter from this point forward.

Inform Your "Troops"

In the Marine Corps, if an officer does not inform his troops, they will inform themselves—usually with unsubstantiated rumor. "Scuttlebutt," the universal term for the kind of hearsay that travels throughout the enlisted ranks with the speed of light, can be harmless, or it can be destructive. For Marines who long for a night on the town, a false rumor that "liberty" is being canceled can needlessly lower morale. For Marines who are about to go into action, false rumors about the enemy or about the mission can be deadly distractions. Fortunately, nothing will squelch a rumor faster than an officer who has never lied to his men.

Marines who know that their officers will be open with them, whether the news is good or bad, will be much less inclined to believe scuttlebutt. Like all human beings, they long for the truth. If they are about to lay their lives on the line, they are entitled to the truth. Marine Corps officers, therefore, hide the truth from the enemy, but not from their own men. All information that is pertinent to the mission is shared with the troops. If the news is bad, they will nod their heads soberly, then help their officers come up with a solution. If the officer is killed, no secrets that could affect the survival of his unit perish with him.

In the workplace, scuttlebutt abounds—usually because the "bad news" is withheld from the employees. Newsletters may trumpet every corporate triumph, but news of disasters (e.g., major contracts lost, stock market slides, supply shortages) is generally communicated in whispers. Often, employees who have just joined the company are dismayed to find that their new boss was less than forthcoming in the final interview. Sales reps are turned loose into a territory they find is full of snakes. Clerks are led to believe a performance bonus will be issued at year's end, only to receive the standard paycheck. In extreme cases, companies go into bankruptcy without telling their employees—all because management was afraid to share the bad news.

Probably the most common mistake made by management is keeping silent while the workplace buzzes with speculation, perhaps out of a conviction that official comment needlessly elevates the status of a rumor. But prolonged official silence is, in fact, what confirms the suspicions of the employees. They ask themselves, "Why isn't the company denying this story?" And the conclusion seems obvious: "because it must be true." Ideally, in the proper environment of openness and trust, the employees would not be bothered by every other rumor that comes down the pike. The best way to create a sense of trust in management is to simply share the bad news. If a major contract is lost, the employees deserve to hear about it "from the top." The reasons for the setback should be discussed frankly and openly. When properly presented by management, a battle lost can motivate the workforce, in much the same way that an officer's bad news can inspire his troops towards a solution.

Rumors, unfortunately, do not stay inside the boundaries of the workplace; they fly outside to the competition, the customers, the stockholders, and to the lenders. All of this can be avoided by a manager who keeps his people informed. The policy of sharing information from the top down can have a profound effect on the workforce. For one thing, employees are very gratified to be told what is going on in the world outside their own assembly bench or office cubicle. They feel more important than their position justifies. Even though they had nothing to do with the decisions being made, they are pleased—as we all would be—that management thinks enough of them to keep them informed.

Imagine two organizations in competition—one whose workforce trusts management to keep it fully abreast of relevant news within the industry, the other a company rife with speculation and distrust. Which one would you bet on to prevail in the marketplace? The trusting relationship described is not difficult to cultivate. All management has to do is tell the truth to the "troops," even if it hurts.

Semper Fit

One of the most distinguishing characteristics of the Marine Corps officer is his physical fitness. One can see at a glance that he is in the best shape of his life. And this goes pretty much across the board; Marine Corps officers of all ranks have the same flat-bellied "runner's" look—as if the Corps were trying to save money by issuing only one size uniform. As officers, they are not excused from the rigorous physical fitness tests taken by NCOs and must test biannually. But this is not their only motivation; being in shape is a matter of manhood. On a ten-mile, hilly cross-country run, the Marine Corps officer must "lead" his troops in the literal sense of the word—he must be in front of the column. The troops behind him, sobbing for oxygen, see only his back. And they think, "if he can do it, I can." An officer who cannot stay in front of his men will never have their respect.

There is also an unspoken competition between the NCOs and the officers. A ten-mile run is cruelly equitable; either you can do it, or you can't. There is no possibility of faking it. Rank doesn't help; it only allows you to publicly raise your arm in surrender, calling the run to a halt. An officer and his sergeant will involuntarily eye each other during these kinds of endurance tests, each reluctant to be the first to show signs of exhaustion.

Top Sergeant Andy Brown, arguably the most successful

Marine Corps recruiter on the planet, remembers his first meeting with newly assigned commanding officer, Lieutenant Colonel William Leek. "He came up here on a day when we were going to run the 'poolees' [recruits on a delayed entry program] up Heartbreak Hill. It was a real hot day. I wanted to see what the colonel was made of, so I pointed out the mountain top that was our goal and asked him if he'd like to come along." Top Sergeant Brown, who himself looks as fit as a fiddle, laughs. "All we saw was the colonel's dust. He beat us all to the top and was doing knuckle pushups on the rocks when the rest of us staggered up." Brown was so impressed with his new CO that he signed up for another tour of duty, even though he had been considering retiring.

Officers compete not only with the men but also among themselves. In a downsizing organization, with fewer and fewer opportunities for advancement, every advantage must be pressed. And physical fitness plays an almost disproportionate role—considering the mechanization of the modern military—in distinguishing one officer from another for promotion. Even colonels and generals try to look a little trimmer than their classmates. In fact, the older officers are in their own way more impressive than the younger ones. Those older, wiser, fifty-year-old faces on top of twenty-five-year-old physiques really add to the overall look of readiness every Marine Corps combat unit exudes.

Business leaders, competing as they do in a very image-conscious environment, would do well to emulate the Marine Corps officer's flat-bellied, trim physique. The obvious health benefits aside, managers who look prepared to "go to the mat" over a business deal tend to impress customers and competitors alike. The suggestion of physical power still has an impact, even in the most civilized negotiations. During the Cold War, President Lyndon Johnson's bone-crushing handshake (delivered with a diplomatic smile) is credited with having had a profound effect on Soviet Prime Minister Andrei Gromyko, who reported to his superiors, after a UN summit meeting, that the Americans were not to be trifled with.

Managers, like Marines, represent something larger than themselves. In the customer's eye, they are personifications of the company that employs them. It may be unjust, but customers cannot help associating the positive or negative characteristics of the person before them with the organization they represent. An overweight sales manager, for example, gives the impression of being employed by a similarly bloated corporation. Conversely, a trim physique reflects a lean, competitive, no-frills company that is not trying to get rich off the customer. Because being fit is also evidence of personal self-control and discipline, the customer quite naturally assumes that these qualities prevail in the company that hired this particular person to represent it. Indeed, customers have confessed to being so impressed by the personal attributes of a company's representative that they have actually made the wrong decision, dismissing a superior product because it was presented by a less charismatic individual.

The effect of a manager's personal appearance is far reaching within his own organization. Subordinates do not want to stand next to him and feel like the "before" photograph in an advertisement for a health product, so they begin to take better care of themselves. Lost days due to illness decrease, as do manifestations of stress in the workplace. When the company promotes and supports physical fitness across the board—for example, by sponsoring departmental athletic competitions, and employee basketball leagues and running clubs—the effect can be spectacular. Like the Marine Corps' combat unit, the company—from the CEO down to the mailroom clerk—can give the impression that it is a team that is ready for anything.

Leave the "How" of an Order to the Subordinate

In Officer Candidate School, there is a famous exercise in which the prospective officers are given the assignment of raising a flag pole so that it meets a number of detailed specifications. It is assumed in the exercise that the officer has one sergeant and two privates to assist him. The instructors are constantly amazed at the ingenuity of the trainees, who have come up with a thousand and one ways to erect that flagpole. What the instructors are looking for, however, is a much simpler answer: "Tell the sergeant to raise the flagpole and walk away."

Officer candidates learn quickly to rely on their sergeants to come up with the "how to" of an order. Of course, the officer is available for friendly advice, but only if the sergeant comes to him for it. Chances are, he won't. Allowing his subordinate to provide the solution is not a shirking of leadership; it is, in fact, quite the reverse. The officer's duty is to cultivate the leadership qualities of all who report to him. It would be a disservice to the sergeant—a veteran Marine with years of practical experience under his belt, as well as countless hours of classroom training—to instruct him on how to carry out an order. Carrying out an order is the sergeant's job; ordering him to do it is the job of the officer, who in turn, must carry out the orders of his own superiors. In each case, the subordinate is free to use his gray matter, so that virtually every order increases his professional capacity—just as every order accompanied with detailed instructions on how to accomplish it would decrease his capacity.

There are occasions when an officer will ask to see a plan of action before he gives his Marines the go-ahead. Here, too, he leaves the plan to his subordinates, who come back with a paragraph or a few pages, depending upon the complexity of the order, describing how they intend to carry it out. The officer reviewing the plan may ask a leading question, such as "Have you considered this possibility?," and allow his men to modify the plan accordingly. But he will not instruct his Marines on how to accomplish the mission.

This policy holds true even in the combat environment. When combat is imminent, the officer's men are still expected to come up with effective plans to carry out the mission. In the confusion that accompanies actual combat, these plans, no matter how well considered, might be suddenly rendered obsolete. In that case, the individual closest to the breach—

officer, sergeant, or private—must make immediate modifications, a task that would be impossible without a personal history of having had to think for himself. Many a Marine Corps officer owes his very life to the policy of cultivating the leadership qualities within all of his men, by letting them come up with the solutions.

Similarly, many a manager owes his job to the resourcefulness of his subordinates. Whenever he is "rescued" by his own staff, the manager should beam with satisfaction—not simply because the crisis is over but because he has been doing his job well, bringing out the leadership qualities of those around him. Every manager who has a policy of allowing his own people to come up with the "how to" of a directive is doing a service to himself, his people, and his company by creating self-confidence and independence within the ranks. Conversely, those who provide detailed instructions with every order breed dependency. In times of crisis, his own people overwhelm him with appeals for guidance.

Thinking for oneself is not a switch that can simply be turned on when the urgent need arises; it is a skill that must be developed over the years. Employees—especially those who are not in love with their jobs—prefer to be led. They may follow competently enough, but, when the time comes for independent and creative action, they are at a loss. The mental skills and the courage to carry out the ideas that may occur to them have not been developed sufficiently. Their managers have failed them by asking for obedience over the years, rather than solutions.

Prepare Your Subordinates for Two Jobs—Theirs and Yours

"I must prepare my "exec" for two jobs—his and mine," says Colonel Richard J. Dallaire, a twenty-eight-year veteran. "We may go into combat, and I might get killed. Suddenly, he's in charge."

This grim scenario is the basis for the Marine Corps' policy of leadership cultivation. In combat emergencies, privates to colonels can suddenly be expected to fill the shoes of their respective superiors immediately. Civilians can only imagine how unnerving that must be. The very person you depended upon to get you out of a dangerous predicament is killed or incapacitated before your eyes; suddenly your men are looking to you for the command decisions.

Fortunately, legitimate business is never a matter of life and death (if it's become that, you really need this book). Nonetheless, there is a corporate mission to fulfill that goes beyond the individuals responsible for carrying it out. The players can change (one hopes, for less dramatic reasons than death!), and the "next in line" may find himself without the guidance of his predecessor. If the corporation does not have a policy of preparing for such contingencies, momentum can be lost at the worst possible time, such as during a major negotiation.

Managers can prepare their subordinates to take charge in a number of ways—some gentle, some not so gentle. On the more comfortable end of the spectrum, a manager can call in his "right-hand man" for advice and counsel on a business dilemma and ask, "What would you do in this situation?" A simple friendly chat like this can have training benefits out of all proportion to the casual setting. The manager gets a peek into the subordinate's method of thinking, while the subordinate sees for himself the kinds of challenges his boss must face. The office becomes a simulation room; and the experience is accepted by the subconscious of the assistant as a "real" experience. By thinking the problem through, he is preparing himself to one day sit at his boss's desk. For his part, the boss has a sounding board for his own ideas and may come away from the conversation with a whole new strategy.

A more shocking way for a manager to introduce his second in command to the responsibilities of the next level is to simply tell him that he must take on the next major presentation or report. This is not meant to be a way of off-loading one's own responsibilities; it is, rather, a simulation of the sudden loss of leadership. The subordinate who must now step up to the plate will be learning some very valuable lessons. He will have to find a way to juggle more than one ball, while dealing with this new assignment in addition to his own pressing responsibilities. He must learn how to do the project suddenly thrust upon him, which is good preparation in itself. And, finally, he will develop an attitude of readiness; if a surprise like this can happen once, it can happen again. For his part, the boss can see how well his next-in-line rises to the occasion.

Encourage Your People to Ask "Why?"

Contrary to the public perception, Marine Corps officers do not do things "by the book" because they believe Marine Corps doctrine to be a sacred text. Actually, during officer training school, the young candidates are encouraged to question the procedures being taught.

"We want our officers to know why we do things the way we do," Major Larry Clayton, an Officer Candidate School Company Commander, explains. "Every tactic we teach has been learned the hard way, on the battlefield. But if you don't know the reasons behind the tactic, you won't be able to appreciate it, or modify it, or pass it on. It's like the monkey experiment."

The "monkey experiment" is a classic laboratory experiment that illustrates exactly what the Marines try to avoid—the thoughtless passing from one group to another of a learned tradition. Six monkeys were put into a cage, in which bananas were suspended by chains. The chains were attached to shower heads so that, when a monkey pulled on the bananas, the entire group received a shower of cold water (like cats, monkeys don't like water). It didn't take long for the six monkeys to learn that the bananas were to be left alone.

A new monkey was then introduced into the group, while one of the original monkeys was removed. Of course, the newcomer saw the bananas and thought it was in monkey paradise. But, as it climbed upward, the five remaining original monkeys would actually prevent it from reaching the bananas. Soon the new monkey, too, learned that the bananas were taboo. Other newcomers were introduced; for each one, a monkey from the original group was removed from the cage. Each time, the group enforced the lesson. Soon, none of the original group was left in the cage, yet the bananas were undisturbed—by monkeys who had never felt the cold shower themselves and who did not know "why" the bananas were to be left alone.

The Marine Corps does not want obedience for its own sake. It is necessary, of course, for officers to follow Marine Corps doctrine, but it is even more important that they know the reasons why the procedures are in place. Once the officer candidate is satisfied on a few issues, he may very well confidently accept the balance, knowing full well that he is always free to ask "why?"

In the world of business, it is even more important to encourage management to question policy and procedures, for this reason: unlike the military, businesses are eager to implement changes, and procedures that are not thoroughly understood may be replaced without due consideration. The lessons that have been learned the hard way over the years and institutionalized in company procedures can be swept away by a CEO who has never taken the time to ask "why?" and who is now doomed to learn these lessons for himself, the hard way.

Don't Be Afraid to Make Things Uncomfortable

No one would describe a career in the Marine Corps as particularly comfortable. It begins with the most arduous basic training to be found on the planet, and the pressure to perform continues throughout one's career. The individual Marine—officer, NCO, or private—is never allowed to fall into a "comfort zone." He must always prepare for the next rank, and, if he fails, he has to leave the Corps. He can't gain weight. He can never rest on past performance. Even at the end of a long and distinguished career, he is forced to compete athletically with Marines young enough to be his children and is expected to either keep pace or retire. He must work in an organization that is continually being downsized, which increases the competition for a reduced number of opportunities up the chain of command. He is not paid very much, compared to his acquaintances in private enterprise. He must travel, often spending extended periods away from his loved ones. When there are hostilities on the other side of the world, he is the first to fight. He wears few medals, because they are awarded infrequently (Marines are expected to be valiant). He lives on bases famous for their lack of amenities. And, if he expects the American public to applaud his sacrifices, he finds that peacetime civilians are benevolently indifferent.

One would expect morale to suffer under these conditions, yet Marines enjoy the highest morale of any branch of the armed forces in the world. Either they are all crazy, or there is something about the difficult life they lead that brings a great deal of satisfaction.

Imagine for a moment a Marine Corps in an "alternate universe," in which the conditions are reversed. In boot camp, recruits are greeted by personal trainers, nutritionists, and supportive psychologists who guide them through three months of athletic activities. There is no Crucible; everyone who signs up becomes a Marine. Promotions are automatic. The pay is proportionately higher than in civilian life. Marine Corps bases are veritable health spas. Medals can be purchased at the PX. Wherever he goes, the Marine is hailed as a conquering hero. Participation in actual war is optional.

Would such a boot camp offer the life-altering transformation we see today? Would such an organization be, in reality, a tight-knit organization of men prepared to fight and die for each other? Obviously, the very stresses of life in the Marine Corps are critical to its legendary esprit de corps. Why is it, then, so many major corporations—which must be victorious in the market or perish—try so hard to "de-stress" the workplace?

Corporations go to great lengths to create a pleasant working environment, on the assumption that happy, comfortable employees will be productive employees. Ergonomic studies guide companies in their choice of furniture, carpet, and color schemes. Agreeable paintings and prints decorate the walls. The light refrain of soothing music is heard throughout the office.

In this pleasant setting, every corporate communiqué reminds the employees that the company is "one big family." And soon they expect to be treated like family. Managers tiptoe around a secretary who is having a "bad hair day." An R&R (rest and relaxation) day is granted to virtually any "stressed-out" employee who asks for it. In the assembly area, workers lounge on their breaks in the company-provided recreation room, playing darts or shooting pool. If an assembler loses his temper and shouts an obscenity on the line, his manager—with visions of a violent employee rampage in mind—rushes over and soothes the unhappy man as if he were a human time bomb.

This emphasis on workplace comfort puts the manager in a difficult position. He wants to spur performance in his department but doesn't want anyone to fear for his job. Under a tremendous amount of stress himself, he has read that poise under pressure is the hallmark of leadership and so internalizes all of his anxiety behind a smiling, public face. On the rare occasions when he does raise his voice in frustration, his subordinates are shocked, hurt, and confused.

Contrast the environment just described with a Marine Corps "workplace." Instead of a smiling receptionist, Marines reporting for duty are greeted by a sergeant, who may or may not be smiling. There is no music in the office; the furniture has initials carved in it. The only things on the walls are Marine motivational posters. In this office, secretaries do not have "bad days." And if a Marine were to lose his temper and curse, he would be reprimanded rather than soothed. His officer, incidentally, is not afraid of workplace violence, even though every Marine under his command is armed to the teeth. And if the officer or NCO raises his voice in anger, no one is shocked or hurt—it's just the "old man" letting off some steam.

We are not suggesting corporate managers should treat their employees like combat-ready Marines. We are suggesting, however, that managers should not be afraid to make things a little uncomfortable for their subordinates now and then—as long as their best interests are kept at heart. When Marine Corps officers, NCOs, and drill instructors are tough on their people, it is for a reason; they want the individual to change, and they want the transformation to come from the inside out. Since periods of change are generally uncomfortable, the individual, as he grows, does experience anxiety and stress. The Marine officer or D.I. does not step in to comfort him during this transformation, even though he may yearn to do so. The recruit, or even a more experienced subordinate, must reach down, deep into his own resources, without much help or encouragement. But eventually, he no longer needs a lot of help or encouragement; he has become independent, resourceful, and definitely more useful to the Marine Corps and to the nation. It is at this point that he finds that his officer, NCO, or D.I. is grinning at him with approval.

When a business manager wants one of his people—who has so far not responded to repeated patient attempts at mentoring—to develop into a more independent, self-motivated professional, he may have to occasionally withhold his guidance. An inadequate report, for example, can be sent back to the subordinate with the word "Unacceptable" written across the top but without suggestions for improvement, forcing him to think long and hard on his own. The individual's work performance can be critiqued in a decidedly frank manner, behind closed doors, during frequent reviews. Since no one likes to see another person uncomfortable, the manager may yearn to sprinkle some of his criticism with positive remarks, but, like the Marine officer, he refrains for the individual's own good. The positive remarks will come later. And when they do come—at the right time and for the right reasons—the compliments will be cherished.

A Marine has no illusions about the expectations of his commanding officer—he is expected to be a warrior. He is of no use to the organization, or to the country, if he cannot contribute to the overall mission of the Marine Corps, which is to win America's battles. Corporations have a mission as well; they must win on the battlefield of the marketplace. Every member of the organization should, like the Marine, have no illusions about his job. No matter how well business may be going on a given day, the company is engaged in a fight for its life. While a pleasant place to work, the company is not a "home" to its employees. Managers, while friendly enough, are not Mommy and Daddy. Everyone from the CEO down is a corporate soldier and is of use only to the degree that they contribute to achieving the mission of the company. Constructive managers who occasionally make things "uncomfortable" for their subordinates do so only to increase their professional capacity. Months or years later, they will be thanked for it.

Stick to the Promotional Ladder—No Skipping Billets

In the Marine Corps, the path to advancement is open to all, but all who travel it must go step by step. No matter how much of a rising star a brilliant officer appears to be, he must start at the first level of command. A platoon commander becomes a company commander on his way up to command a battalion, then a regiment. At each step up the ladder, he learns valuable lessons for the next level of responsibilities.

The command path is strictly enforced by the Marine Corps. Even after an officer has been approved by the Promotion Board, a separate, autonomous Command Board will evaluate his fitness to lead more Marines. It is unheard of for an officer who has never commanded a battalion to be allowed to command a regiment. The Marine Corps will never let an officer reach too high for a post—his feet must be planted firmly on the foundation of experience.

In the corporate world, even the rising star should be made to experience the challenges of command at each level within the organization. Allowing him to skip a step is a disservice both to him, and to the company itself. Each successful command experience is an accreditation for the next level; skipping a level weakens the structure of one's career from that point on. Just as each floor of a skyscraper rests firmly on the floor below—all the way down to the bedrock—a manager's totality of experience should logically and inexorably lead to his present level of responsibilities.

We use the term "career path" because it implies a journey; and the journey toward increased professional capacity is fraught with pitfalls. The veteran manager avoids these pitfalls only because he has fallen before, earlier in his career, at a time when the consequences were proportionate to his responsibilities and therefore less serious. If those learning experiences had been forfeited because of a manager's meteoric rise within the chain of command, that manager's next stumble could be consequential indeed.

There are occasions, of course, when the best person for the job must be brought in from another company. It should be made clear to the incoming manager that he is expected to learn the particulars of the company through an accelerated "apprenticeship" in the positions he would have served in had he been with the company a few years. After a month or two of a "virtual career," learning the ropes from those in the posts he would have served in under normal circumstances, the manager will be much more competent to begin the job he was hired to do. He will also realize that, from this point on, there will be no skipping of billets.

Don't Fraternize With the "Troops"

All Marine Corps officers make it a point to get to know their men as well as is practically possible—given the numbers that may be under their command—but actual fraternization is scrupulously avoided. The tradition that prohibits close relationships between the officer and the men he commands, like all Marine Corps traditions, evolves from putting the mission—which is winning battles—first and foremost. Marine Corps reasoning goes like this: fraternization leads to favoritism; favoritism in combat reduces combat efficiency; therefore, fraternization reduces combat efficiency.

Marine Corps officers must guard against the very human tendency to like one individual more than another. In combat, the officer's decisions must be totally objective—even with regard to his own life. If an officer had to agonize over ordering a close personal friend into danger, the success of the mission would be jeopardized. It would also be unpardonable to protect one's friend by sending another, less well-liked, individual into harm's way. Even in the noncombat environment, fraternization is totally unacceptable. Officers must be the veritable statue of Justice, blindfolded in their duty assignments, or unit morale will suffer. Every Marine is entitled to, and expects, absolute fairness from his superiors. The moment an officer's objectivity is doubted, he will lose the respect of his men. And nothing worse could possibly happen to a Marine officer. The army may "travel on its stomach," but the Marine Corps travels on mutual respect.

While all officers have the legal authority to command, the moral authority to lead is not granted by a diploma from Officers Candidate School. Moral authority is developed in private, with one's conscience, and on display in public, in the day-to-day dealings with the men under one's command. An officer with legal authority can expect his orders to be followed to the letter, but perhaps no further. The officer with moral authority may find that his men will go far beyond the call of duty, perhaps to their deaths, upon his order. This is why he will never tarnish the character he has assiduously built up within himself. An officer who decides to be "one of the boys," even for one night, and gets falling down drunk with his troops will never be looked upon with the same degree of respect again. No matter how dignified he tries to appear the following day, his men will see only the party buffoon.

The consequences of fraternization with the men under his command may be somewhat localized; the morale of the platoon may suffer, but the Marine Corps itself (at least temporarily), and certainly the general public, will be unaware. Fraternization with the women under his command, however, can literally become front-page news. Several scandals involving the other branches of the armed forces have already alerted the American public to the fact that sexual harassment is not exclusive to private enterprise. Parents who were once enthusiastic over the prospect of their daughters joining the military now wonder if Uncle Sam can be trusted. Marine Corps officers and NCOs are very sensitive to this issue and scrupulously avoid even the appearance of special consideration for a Marine of the opposite sex. Unlike the other branches of the armed forces, the Marines do not integrate women recruits with men during basic training. And, although the army, navy, and air force allow marriages between their officers and enlisted personnel—as long as one is not under the direct command of the other—Marines in the same situation can't even date.

In the corporate environment, in which it is impossible not to fraternize with one's associates, the manager's challenges are even greater than those facing the Marine officer. Managers are expected to be friendly and open, and there are more opportunities to socialize. And male and female associates do not walk around in dungarees and combat boots. There is also, simultaneously, a greater sensitivity to perceived favoritism. Unlike the Marine Corps, the workplace environment is not one of self-sacrifice. Employees are motivated much more by self-interest than by the collective good and are not shy about asking, "Why did he or she get this assignment and not me?"

It goes without saying that close relationships and office romances with subordinates directly under one's authority should be strictly avoided. Sexual harassment lawsuits have ruined the careers of managers, have embittered employees, and have caused costly and totally unnecessary distractions from the corporate goal of victory in the marketplace. The morale of an entire office can be adversely affected by the perception that a manager is favoring one individual—especially if the favoritism seems to stem from qualities unrelated to work performance. It is tremendously unfair for any manager to bestow favors upon a subordinate for subjective reasons. He will lose in short order the respect and loyalty of those under his authority—a condition that will soon be apparent to the powers above.

The manager had better have irrefutable, objective reasons for his appointments and promotions or he may have a silent revolt on this hands, if not actual litigation. He will find, however, that challenges to his decisions will decrease in inverse proportion to the esteem in which he is held. Employees who trust in the objectivity of their manager's judgments will not feel that appeals are necessary or even worthwhile—unless they have a strictly rational argument. A manager who does not allow himself to be swayed by his own emotional biases will be unmoved by ardent but unsubstantiated appeals for special consideration from his subordinates. Like the Marine officer, he will never allow his own behavior to interfere with the "mission readiness" of his department."

Motivate Those in Unhappy Slots

The Marine Corps, like private enterprise, offers a vast selection of occupational specialties. Recruiters go to great pains to identify an individual's talents and even guarantee training schools and assignments; after all, the Marine Corps wants its people to make a career of it. But there will always be individuals who have no clear idea of what they want to do and also those who discover that they have made the wrong choice of duty stations. Unlike in private enterprise, however, a Marine can't simply quit and look for a more enjoyable job. So, there are times when an officer must motivate an unhappy Marine.

Indeed, there are times when the officer himself wishes he were somewhere else.

The Marine Corps is very sensitive to this issue and does its best to sweeten the pot for unpopular assignments. As mentioned earlier, a tour of recruiting duty is not what most young men join the Corps for. Combat-ready infantrymen who suddenly find themselves having to learn sales techniques and public speaking skills, and saddled with a monthly quota of quality recruits, are not always happy they accepted the assignment of recruiter. The Marine Corps responds by elevating this unpopular post to one of the most important tours of duty a Marine can have. Promotion is virtually guaranteed at the end of a successful three-year hitch. In addition, only the cream of the crop is even asked to be recruiters; those who accept must grudgingly admit to being flattered. And, finally, recruiters are paid slightly more than their peers, ostensibly to offset their dry-cleaning bills (recruiters are in "dress blues" a lot).

For the unpopular assignment that does not carry with it the promise of promotion—such as guarding a lonely outpost in the middle of nowhere—the officer praises his men for doing a job that is important in the overall scheme of things and one that will be highlighted in their service records. And, in the most "unhappy" position of all—being pinned down by enemy machine gun fire—the officer motivates with his own displays of confidence in the end result.

Business managers, fortunately, do not have to lead their personnel through combat, except perhaps in cases of workplace rampages, but they are often called upon to motivate those who are unhappy in their current slots. There are any number of reasons for employee discontent. Some must work the "graveyard shift," or on weekends. Employees are occasionally transferred from their homes to remote facilities. Some are called upon to pioneer a new marketplace, where the company is unknown. Some have been denied a lateral move they coveted; some may have to work with a difficult associate who has been with the company for too many years to simply terminate. Here again, the manager can learn a lot from the Marine Corps officer.

When an employee who is unhappy with his assignment asks, "Why me?," the answer should be, "Because you're my best man." Few will disagree with that statement, as long as it is delivered with sincerity. The manager should point out the high visibility of the assignment, reminding the individual that he is in a position to be a hero. The position can be linked with a promotion, for all the company to see. Like the Marine officer, the manager can appeal to the sense of duty: "This job is critically important to the company, and I need someone I can trust." He can sweeten the pot with the business equivalent of "hazardous duty pay." And, like the Marine officer, he must never abandon one of his own to an ignominious position. By keeping in close touch, he reminds the employee that he is important, that his efforts are greatly appreciated, and that his boss is in the trenches with him.

Repeat Orders

Boot camp is a very noisy place. Drill instructors seem to be always shouting at someone a few blocks away, even while addressing the hapless recruit only inches from his thrusting face. Of course, the D.I. wants his comments to be overheard by the rest of the platoon under his charge, but the sheer volume of his voice, combined with a truly unpleasant expression, is also designed to scare the recruit right out of his socks. No matter how loudly a recruit answers, he can never seem to make himself heard. "I can't hear you!" screams the D.I. And the recruit tries again, in an even louder attempt. With all the yelling going on, one would think that listening would be easy.

The average recruit, however, initially goes straight into shock when the drill instructor bellows at him. It is all he can do to come up with an adequate "Yes, Sir!" But his D.I. wants specifics. "What did I say?" asks the screaming voice. And the recruit who cannot repeat, word for word, the injunctions of his D.I. will soon be doing knuckle pushups, or some such punishment. Often a squad of twelve will line up, with a drill instructor at either end. One D. I. will whisper a message into the ear of the end recruit, who in turn will whisper it to the man next to him, so that the message goes through the ears and lips of all twelve recruits. The D.I. at the opposite end awaits the final interpretation and God help that squad if he does not hear the exact, agreed-upon wording initiated by the D.I. at the front of the line.

There is a method to all Marine Corps madness and, whether the recruit realizes it or not, his very life may one day depend upon a crystal-clear understanding of an order shouted to him on the battlefield. He may have to execute that order or pass it along without the slightest embellishment; in either case, the communication process must be pure. But the surest way to know that one's intentions have been clearly understood is to have a policy of repetition. A Marine is asked to repeat the order just given. He is not offended by the request; if he has misunderstood an order he wants to be the first to know. Throughout his career, he will voluntarily repeat his orders to the originator and require the same from his subordinates. Every Marine who issues a command wants to be sure, before the other walks away, that they are both of one mind. This is why Marine artillerymen repeat aloud the ranges called out by the range finder and why Marine pilots repeat, word for word, the instructions of their air traffic controllers (as do commercial pilots, incidentally). Over time, every Marine learns that life is much easier if he simply pays attention when someone is talking to him and then verbalizes his own understanding. By that simple practice, he never has to walk away wondering, "What did the officer say?"

The repetition of orders may appear unnecessarily redundant to those of us in business. Provided there are other mechanisms in place to ensure that instructions are clearly comprehended, perhaps it is redundant. But, what are these other measures? Asking a person if he "understands" is no safeguard—all of us have at one time or another nodded in the affirmative when we were actually in doubt, not wanting to appear inattentive or stupid. And if the instructions are issued in a snappy, hurried manner, we want to mirror the urgency of the situation and immediately go into action—often without a clear understanding of the desired end result.

In fact, "hurry" is really one of the most common obstacles to communication. Most of us have had the experience of asking a busy receptionist to repeat the message we have just left and then been shocked at the interpretation. Ironically, the receptionist may not even have been particularly busy; the desire to appear efficient under stress makes us accelerate unnecessarily. Not only is communication jeopardized, the people we deal with feel shortchanged.

Managers, by facial expression and body language, can unknowingly appear impatient, which of course discourages questions and prompts subordinates to "force" an understanding upon their own minds. The manager who is demonstrably pleased by questions and delighted by the opportunity to clarify his intentions will save himself much grief. The employee is often at fault, as well; he can give the impression that there is no need to tell him anything twice and that he would consider it an insult to be asked, like a child, to repeat his instructions. In this case, the manager simply has to use a little tact. He might say, "My wife tells me I don't always make myself very clear; what's your understanding of what has to be done?" or ask, "If you had to repeat this to Tom, what would you say?"

The manager can, like the Marine Corps officer, also ask for a written plan. It doesn't have to be anything formal, perhaps a simple paragraph or two indicating how the subordinate intends to carry out his "mission." It will be immediately apparent if there has been a miscommunication. There is also the very real possibility that, even though the instructions have been misunderstood, the employee has really come up with a clever idea. But, whether it is written or verbal, some kind of evidence must be submitted to show that the subordinate truly understands what must be done. As long as it becomes a matter of policy, the employee will not feel singled out. Eventually he may get "in the habit" and, like the Marine, voluntarily repeat his orders. It's a habit that works well in the Marine Corps and, perhaps slightly modified, would work well in the corporation—where clear communication is just as important.

Of course, managers must first make sure that they themselves understand the directive from on high. After repeating the order back to the boss or to the customer, it is essential to confirm in writing, via letter, fax, or e-mail. When the order is passed down and backed up "with paper," it is a good idea to randomly ask a number of employees how they interpret the directive. Not only will the manager discover if his message has gotten through, he will soon find out if the very system of communication is in need of repair. Nothing will be learned, however, unless the manager always assumes that his or her directives are fragile things, open to misinterpretation. Corporate soldiers, like Marines, must frequently be asked to express, by reiteration or by plan, their understanding of what has to be done.

Build a Team

No organization stresses self-reliance more than the Marine Corps, and no organization teaches teamwork with greater emphasis. This apparent contradiction is easily resolved: Marines must first be as independently resourceful as possible in order to contribute toward—and not rely upon—their team. The entire boot camp experience is simultaneously a process of self-discovery—as each recruit must reach deep into his own inner resources to endure its challenges—and an initiation into the group consciousness. A recruit learns that he must succeed individually to be of use to his fire team (of three Marines), his squad (of four fire teams), his platoon (of four squads), and so on. But it is the team that gets the job done. That's why every event in basic training is designed to promote teamwork.

Even one of the most traditionally "single-handed" events has been modified to create a team consciousness and fighting spirit. Years ago, when the authors attended boot camp, pugil stick fighting (simulated bayonet fighting) was definitely a "one-on-one" challenge. Two individuals from different platoons, wearing football helmets, would face off and, at the blow of a whistle, fight each other with the padded pugil stick, until one received a "lethal" blow. Today, teams of recruits clash in the pugil stick circle so that one learns not to just fight for himself but for his buddy as well. If his buddies are "killed," the remaining recruit must defend himself against multiple attackers, who close in intelligently, as a team. Thus, teamwork is taught while defending and attacking.

In daily military life, in maneuvers, and in combat, the mission is accomplished because Marines are working together. Through constant training, they have seen for themselves how much more a team can achieve. But that does not make Marines cocky; the sense of increased power each individual feels as part of the team is counter-balanced by his obligation to contribute as much as is personally possible. The Marine Corps tries its best to keep the teams together for an entire tour of duty; the bonding grows stronger with each maneuver and with each Friday night on the town. If sent into combat, the twelve Marines in a squad look out for one another as if they were a family.

In the corporate environment, "teamwork" is the buzzword of management. It is used in every communication to the rank and file. Motivational posters of individuals joining forces and working together are hung on the walls of offices and production areas in virtually every business in the country. "Teamwork" is promoted at every opportunity. But where are the actual teams?

In many corporate environments, despite all the hype about working together, teams are hard to find. If the team concept is actually implemented, it is usually only at the top. "Team selling," for example, is reserved for the most important customers, while smaller accounts are handled by the individual salesperson. "Team production" is a reality on some assembly lines, but, there again, usually only for the big-ticket items such as automobiles; the lone worker doing the identical repetitive chore is still the norm in many industries. Maybe it is impractical to have teams of specialists bursting into the office of every small account, or for a group of assemblers to crowd around a miniature integrated circuit board, but the Marine Corps' team concept can certainly be applied to every level of the organization, including the lowest.

In fact, the psychological energy derived from working together must flow from the bottom up. Team spirit in the Marine Corps begins with the three young privates in a fire team; their enthusiasm joins with the energy of the other fire teams and swells horizontally and vertically throughout the rank and file into an esprit de corps that should be the envy of any organization. But it is important to note that the morale at the bottom—the three-man fire team—is just as high as it is at the top—a brigade or regiment— it's just not quite as loud.

Employees who by necessity must work alone can still be an integral part of a team, in terms of their contribution toward collective goals. Enthusiastic managers can build team spirit in the most unlikely working environments by simply making each individual feel simultaneous emotions of gratitude and obligation toward his fellow employees. Just as individual Marines compete with each other, not for personal recognition but in an almost sacrificial effort to give to the team, employees can be encouraged to think beyond themselves. Team recognition and reward will warm the most cynical heart; and, if they don't—if the individual is tempted instead to rely upon his team, rather than "repay" it with his own effort—the manager must take the individual aside.

On whatever level of the organization, the team must never be a haven for its members. Marine Corps teams, in maneuvers or in combat, are aggressive; they move forward. The Marines in a squad or platoon may provide cover for each other, but the unit is not obsessed with protecting itself; completion of the mission is always the goal. If anything, teams encourage aggression (or, in business parlance, "competitive attitude") because each member is reluctant to be fearful in front of his teammates. If a manager hears his team come up with collective excuses for not meeting its goals, then he might as well have a group of individuals working for him.

Encourage Peer Evaluations

In Chapter 2, we described boot camp for the rank-and-file enlisted Marine. Officer basic training, while less well known, is as, if not more, difficult. Officer boot camp is, however, distinctive in that (1) the officer "recruit" can drop out whenever he wants, and (2) during the training, much use is made of "peer evaluations." The first distinction already applies to the world of free enterprise, but we would guess that many companies have not considered the benefits of asking, or requiring, employees to appraise each other.

Marine Corps officer candidates are, of course, carefully monitored and assessed by their drill instructors throughout basic training. And the difficulty of the training itself generally (but not always) identifies those individuals who will not make it through. But peer evaluations provide another mechanism for determining which individuals have the proper mental, physical, and psychological characteristics that qualify them for leading America's Finest.

Jokingly referred to as "spear evaluations," the observations made by a candidate's fellows are based upon a much more intimate view of the candidate than that of the instructor's. As colleagues, they witness each other's private sides during what little private time there is in basic training. They know, for example, if an officer candidate studies at night under the blanket with a flashlight, or if he does pushups on his own time to build strength. Conversely, they know if he is a chronic complainer once out of earshot of the drill instructor, or if he does not maintain, in private, his "public" enthusiasm.

Peer evaluations have the added benefit of drawing out of the individual an extra measure of performance. He doesn't just have to convince his drill instructors that he has what it takes to lead Marines; he has to convince his fellow would-be officers, as well; and they are around him every moment of the day and night. The pressure really never lets up. The only time an officer candidate has for himself is literally in his dreams; and it's a safe bet the grim visage of his drill instructor intrudes there, as well.

One would think that, as sympathetic buddies, the officer recruits might be tempted to take it easy on one another in their respective evaluations. But the drill instructors make it clear that the stakes are very high. If the wrong man is allowed to lead Marines into battle, the lives of his command may be needlessly lost. So an officer candidate's fellow recruits, filled with the sense of righteousness that boot camp tends to create, feel morally obligated to be candid in their appraisals. If anything, peer evaluations may be harsher than those of the drill instructors (who take that into consideration).

Peer evaluations in the corporation can be of great value to all levels of management and in fact can be useful throughout the rank and file, for the very same reasons they are solicited in Marine Corps officer training. One's associates are not as easily impressed as one's manager; they see the "real" person eight hours a day, away from the limelight. In fact, peer evaluations take away the defense of the employee who vociferously disagrees with his manager's appraisal of him—on the grounds that managers are too removed from the "trenches" to accurately evaluate such qualities as initiative and organizational skills. What defense is possible when one's own co-workers agree with the observations of the boss?

Team members, especially, should be asked to critique one another, because they are the ones who suffer directly from an associate's lack of effort or focus, and they are the ones who can help him. Conversely, it is in their self-interest to praise a deserving member so that management is not tempted to break up the team. Not to be confused with "tattle-taleing," peer evaluations are meant to be constructive. In fact, by formalizing the process, the destructive "peer evaluations" that are already practiced in most companies—in the form of whispers, gossip, and sly remarks—tend to abate. Once an associate must commit his comments in writing, he becomes more thoughtful. Aware that he himself is being written about, he anticipates what another may say of his own faults and tries to correct them ahead of time. Even if management takes all of these reports and dumps them, unread, into the wastebasket, it will notice a collective boost in overall performance.

Should peer evaluations be anonymous or signed? In the Marine Corps, they are signed, which no doubt has a sobering effect on the author of the report. Malicious or spurious comments are less likely to appear, being replaced by thoughtful suggestions on how the individual can improve. Requiring a signature also has an unexpected benefit—the report becomes a psychological profile of the author. In a sense, he will be evaluated for his own evaluations.

How seriously should peer evaluations be taken? While informative and helpful to the manager, they are not meant to replace his own judgments. Few managers worth their salt would let another person's opinion override his own direct observation, anyway. But a manager might be tempted to pass the buck and refer to an employee's peer evaluations as the cause for disciplinary action or for the refusal of a raise or promotion. Managers must never hide behind peer evaluations; indeed they should rarely reference them at all, except in the most general terms, such as "Your peers think you are a little weak in this area." In today's litigious workplace, in which even the most justifiable punitive actions of the company are challenged by savvy employees, management must avoid all appearances of holding a kangaroo court with a jury composed of one's associates.

To avoid an employee challenge, peer evaluations should be:

1. Prepared by management so that the questions, always phrased in the positive, preclude personal, nonbusiness related judgments
2. Required, so that no one feels persecuted by voluntary "tattle-taleing"

3. Infrequent, so that no one imagines that the company is attempting to build a case against him

If management is uncomfortable with the concept, peer evaluations can still be used as a great motivational tool. Presented as a leadership exercise, the employee-generated report cards can be filled out anonymously and mailed directly to each individual, unread by management. At least this way, everyone will have the benefit of knowing how he is perceived by his associates. And that can be an eye-opening experience.

Be a Teacher-Scholar

The American military at the end of the eighteenth century was modeled closely on the British example, which wasn't a bad idea, considering that Britain at that time, despite its loss of its American colonies, ruled the world. Many British traditions were perpetuated in the American system until comparatively recently, including what amounted to a caste system that separated the officer corps from the rank and file. The phrase "an officer and a gentleman" had a literal significance; officers were gentlemen, in fact they had to be. A military commission was the prerogative of the aristocracy; and it was often awarded arbitrarily to those of blue blood, rather than earned. For some, the officer's uniform was nothing more than a splendid, masculine costume to be worn at gala balls.

At the other end of the social spectrum was the common soldier, who was generally illiterate and without civil grace. Having no trade other than his expertise with the musket and the bayonet, he reentered society after his years of service hoping to exist on a meager pension. The relationship between the two classes was strictly an authoritarian one: the officer gave the orders, and the enlisted man followed. Even in the early Marine Corps—which had a much more robust, rough-and-ready officer corps—the enlisted man was generally not considered "leadership material" and, therefore, a worthwhile investment of the officer's time.

The Marine who mandated a change of attitude in his officer Corps was General John Lejeune, the Commandant of the Marine Corps, who wrote in 1920:

> The World War wrought a great change in the relations between officers and enlisted men in the military services. A spirit of comradeship and brotherhood in arms came into being in the training camps and on the battlefields. This spirit is too fine a thing to be allowed to die. It must be fostered and kept alive and made the moving force in all Marine Corps organizations. (*Fleet Marine Force Manual* 1–0)

General Lejeune could see that the class barriers in the society outside the Marine Corps were falling of their own weight. The enlisted Marine now came from a better-educated, middle-class background. Lejeune recognized in this group a vast source of future leaders. But, in order for this resource to be cultivated, the officer had to become less an unapproachable, authoritarian figure and more a teacher.

Lejeune's "teacher-scholar" philosophy became institutionalized in Marine Corps leadership training. Incoming officers were taught to look upon those under their supervision as students, rather than subordinates. The mission of the Marine Corps positively demanded it. If Marines are to succeed in battle every time, especially under unfavorable circumstances, every Marine must be a leader. The officer, who himself may be killed, cannot afford to be looked upon as the only source of guidance. His knowledge must be distributed throughout the rank and file. By teaching one, who in turn passes the lesson on, he teaches many. This may be one reason why Marines appear to need less supervision than their counterparts in the other branches of the armed forces. The ratio of officers to enlisted men, for example, is nearly half that in the army (one Marine officer to every nine Marines, compared to one army officer to every five soldiers).

One would think that the more democratic environment

of the American corporation would be characterized by the "teacher-scholar" relationship. But many employees feel as if they work within a "boss-subordinate" hierarchy, which offers them little hope of ever being accepted as a peer by management. The door to the manager's office always seems to be closed, metaphorically barring access into what is seen as an exclusive club of corporate leaders. Membership in this club often seems a matter of "who you know," rather than of "what you know." Managers who lunch or golf with each other only reinforce the impression of upper-level solidarity. Whenever the CEO or one of the vice presidents comes to visit the department, he sits with the manager, not the workforce; and there is yet another "closed-door" meeting. The intelligent and ambitious employee may feel shut out, stymied by restricted opportunities for advancement.

A manager who does not take the ambition of his subordinates seriously does great damage to the organization he is supposed to be serving. Instead of cultivating the creativity and initiative of his people, he neglects their potential. And, instead of building leaders who will loyally serve the company, he unwittingly supplies other companies with the talented personnel who will eventually abandon him. Even worse are the managers who *do* recognize the ambition in their subordinates and, fearing the personal competition, intentionally withhold their knowledge and guidance. And worse yet are the managers who think it unseemly or "uppity" for an employee to even harbor an aspiration to become a corporate leader. It is ironic that management, which is always admonishing its people to "reach for the stars" in terms of performance, is often at a loss for words when an employee takes this advice to its logical conclusion and requests a timetable for his entry into the upper level of the organization.

There are other obstacles to the "teacher-scholar" relationship within the workplace. A manager may avoid the role of teacher for fear of exposing his own ignorance. Rather than simply letting down his guard and learning a procedure by actually performing it, along with his personnel, he hides behind the job title and the unavailability of his office. Conversely, employees may not ask to be taught, because they similarly fear exposure. The net result is management by crisis; the inevitable mistakes are made, and the whole department must work overtime to correct them—with both the manager and his personnel drawing unwanted attention from top management.

The boss-subordinate relationship is not in the best interests of the company, any more than it is in the best interests of the Marine Corps. If the company is to prevail over its competition on the "battlefield" of the marketplace, managers, like Marine officers, must look upon their people as leaders in the making. The manager must freely share his expertise—not only about company procedures and products and services but also with regard to the supervisory skills he has worked so hard to acquire. If his attitude is, "Let them go out and get their own MBAs," the personnel under his authority will never have the full benefit of his experience. Without it, they will perform at a lower standard than is possible, jeopardizing the manager's own success. With it, they will require less supervision and serve as evidence of his own ability to inspire and train a competent workforce.

Every manager must ask himself: (1) Do I want my personnel to be the best they possibly can be, even if that means they will compete for my job? (2) Do I think of my people in terms of their having a career in the company? and (3) Do I care about the company's success after I'm gone? All answers will be in the affirmative, we hope, but even if they're not, it is still in the manager's best interest to become a teacher. If he doesn't teach his personnel, somebody else will, for better or for worse.

Leadership Strategies Checklist

—See that every manager feels entitled to lead.
—Ensure that managers can never distance themselves from a subordinate's failure.

—Understand that the wider his perspective, the more effective the leader.
—Lead by personal example.
—Put the concerns of your personnel before any task.
—Keep your people fully informed.
—Personally exemplify mental and physical readiness.
—Encourage and empower your subordinates to find the solution.
—Prepare your subordinates for two jobs—theirs and yours.
—Encourage questions, even in urgent situations.
—Be prepared to occasionally withhold guidance and praise.
—Never promote beyond the next organizational step.
—Avoid close personal relationships with anyone under your authority.
—Be especially motivating to those who are unhappy in their positions.
—Ask for a verbal or written confirmation of your instructions.
—Create a team culture of self-sacrifice.
—Make use of peer evaluations at all levels of management.
—Be a teacher, not a boss.

5

Senior Management: Leading the Organization

"It is a paradox, and a hard reality, that much of what the commander does to execute his responsibilities today will not be measured until well after he or she is gone."
—General Charles Krulak, Commandant, USMC

"The greatest leadership principle I learned in the Marine Corps was the necessity to take care of the troops in a high performance-based organization.

"The Marine Corps' strong emphasis on this overriding leadership requirement has been of inestimable importance to me in developing FedEx over the years. In the main, people want to be committed to an organization and to do a good job. The principles of leadership taught by the USMC, and based on two centuries of experience, will produce outstanding organizational results in any setting, if those principles are studiously followed.

"In short, FedEx owes its success to this simple truth."
—Frederick W. Smith, Chairman of the Board and CEO of FedEx, formerly Captain, USMC

Business magazines often profile chief executives of major corporations as if they bore the world on their shoulders. But, consider for a moment the weight of a general's responsibilities. If he makes a poor battle decision, hundreds may die; even his correct decision may cost scores of American lives. There is a tendency for the public to imagine that generals are immune from the impact of casualty statistics, that they think in terms of "acceptable losses," and that, to them, a platoon may be "expendable." But the general is, of all people, the one most susceptible to the pangs of conscience. True, he has been prepared for the job by a career in the Marines, but that, in a sense, is what makes his decisions so painful. After so many years of association, he is too close to those under his command to order them into combat, yet he must. How many CEOs would be able to live with that kind of responsibility?

At times, a general must choose a course of action upon a moment's notice, without the benefit of the information that historians and "armchair quarterbacks" will have at their disposal, after the fact. A general must know the capabilities of his own organization, at every level, and simultaneously be an expert on the "competition." His mind must retain the "big picture" even though its many elements may be constantly changing. He must be able to manage, administer, and inspire his personnel to a degree to which those of us on the outside cannot fully appreciate.

Business leaders are fond of using the term *command decisions*. We believe they can learn a great deal from the people who really must make command decisions. Fortunately, many of the Marine Corps general's unique leadership skills can be emulated to great success by those in top management.

There Is No Higher Calling

Commandant Krulak has said numerous times, "There is no higher calling than being a Marine." On the face of it, this is an audacious and somewhat antiquated statement. We rarely hear a person nowadays speak in terms of "higher callings," and, when we do, it is usually in a religious context. A man quits his job and enters the ministry because he has had a "higher calling." And, while those of a different faith may not agree with him, the term is tolerated because it refers to the spiritual realm, which is, at least, "high." But when a Marine insists that his is the highest calling, we are taken aback.

Such a bold statement, however, is not without foundation. A Marine has voluntarily chosen an austere way of life, one that puts him in the forefront of danger as "the first to fight." He is a defender of his country's highest values—freedom, democracy, individual rights—and the commitment to these within the Corps approaches religious devotion. So a Marine who says he follows the highest calling may be speaking with better reason than we might at first admit.

Would a business leader dare to make such a statement? If the CEO of IBM proclaimed, "There is no higher calling than being an IBM employee!," his board of directors might think he was in need of a vacation. But, is the statement so far-fetched?

If service to humanity is the standard, then many occupations that produce products or services that improve our lot on earth would qualify as a "high calling." Certainly the products of a company like IBM have helped to raise the quality of life all over the world by quantum leaps. The fact that an employee of IBM, or any other company, works for personal gain only serves to increase his standing; by looking out for himself and his family, he relieves others of that burden.

Given all this, should a CEO proclaim that there is no higher calling than being an employee of his organization? Perhaps not—for fear of being misunderstood—but it's certainly all right to *think* it. In fact, a CEO who does not feel this way should look for another company to manage—one that actually does contribute toward a better life for all. The good news is that there are hundreds of thousands of companies that qualify. When the commandant says, "There is no higher calling than being a Marine," he is not suggesting that being a Marine is the "highest" calling; he is saying, rather, that being a Marine is on par with every other calling in life, including the most noble. Similarly, every corporate leader should communicate to his workforce that its efforts are important and that employees should be very proud of what they do—for the company, for themselves, and, literally, for the world. If any employee is embarrassed to tell his friends what he does for a living, there has been a failure of leadership at his workplace.

Small Can Be Good

The Marine Corps does not object to being the smallest branch of the armed forces; it positively revels in it. Although its leadership always has concerns about downsizing and about getting its fair share of funding from Congress, the fact that the Corps is small is not at all seen as a negative. On the contrary, its comparatively small size is a recruiting lure. The Marine Corps has defined itself as The Few, The Proud. Being part of "the few" distinguishes a Marine from "the many"; and he wouldn't have it any other way. In the history of advertising and marketing, it is doubtful if any other organization has so effectively turned what could have been a negative into a positive.

Operationally, "small" also means more efficient. With fewer levels of bureaucracy, the Marine Corps is much like a machine with fewer moving parts, easier to maintain and more economical to operate. The most compact branch of the armed forces, it is able to react on a moment's notice. Marines are "the first to fight" because they can literally get there sooner than the army. The role of the Marine Corps is the least ambiguous of all the branches of the service. By design, it is the nation's 911 response to emergencies anywhere in the world; its very size allows the military high command to better define its missions.

"Small" is good for the Marine Corps in other ways. Because of its size, there is a great deal of pressure upon the Corps to distinguish itself from the "competition." Marines have to excel; otherwise there would be no compelling reason to maintain a separate branch of the military—a "rapid deployment force" within the army could take over the 911 job. Being small also means lower recruitment quotas, allowing the Marines to be more selective in the recruiting process, especially for its officers.

But small to a business is not usually something to boast about. It is seen as a condition that must be remedied. "Small" is acceptable only as a reference point, to show how "big" the business has now become. A CEO looks back upon the early days of his company in much the same way as he looks upon his own baby photographs—with a kind of uncomfortable incredulity. He would rather talk about the present, in which he and his company are "grown up."

While every CEO is under a mandate to "grow the business," he would be wise to remember the example of the Marine Corps—the smallest service, with the biggest reputation. Thinking "small" is an attitude, a company philosophy that can be maintained whatever the company's size. For example, no matter how large the company becomes, it should remain a "family"; no matter how secure its position in the marketplace, it should solicit its customers with all the deference of an "underdog"; although a Goliath in assets, it must remain a David in attitude. One only has to look at the changing attitude of the media toward Microsoft to see the advantages to being, at least in a public relations sense, a "David." Originally portrayed by the media as a dragon slayer with the courage to take on IBM itself, Microsoft is today regarded by the media as an ominous corporate giant out to capture the entire market for computer operating systems.

Thinking small perpetuates organizational simplicity, as the company grows, so that efficiency does not suffer. Thinking small may prevent a company from going into markets where it really doesn't belong, saving it the pain of divestiture years later. And, as with the Marine Corps, "small" can be a big marketing tool; Avis Rent A Car made a name for itself with the slogan "We're Number Two; We Try Harder."

Create a No-Frills Culture

Even though all military life is comparatively Spartan, there is one branch of the armed forces that offers even fewer amenities than the others. An army, navy, or air force base, while certainly not opulent, at least belongs in the twentieth century. There you will find a nice swimming pool for the families on base, a comfortable theater, a library, even an eighteen-hole golf course. On a Marine Corps base, you might find an outdoor basketball hoop in a far-off corner of the parking lot. Living quarters can be best described as monastic, with half the personal storage space enjoyed by soldiers, sailors, and air force personnel. Instead of air conditioning, the base gyms have fans the size of airplane propellers. In place of state-of-the-art exercise machines, rusty barbells are hoisted by grunting Marines. In virtually every aspect but morale, the Marine Corps base lags behind.

Marines do not, however, feel deprived by the comparative lack of amenities. In fact, they joke about how soft the army, navy, and air force have it. Just being a Marine is the greatest "perk" of all. Their base is a place to prepare for combat. And it looks it.

We are not suggesting that the corporate workplace revert to grim offices and factories out of a Dickens novel. But it is important that upper management realize that, at least in the case of the Marine Corps, morale is not proportionately linked to increased amenities. Consultants would have upper management believe that executives, managers, and employees will not join, or remain with, a company that is behind its competitors in perks and workplace comforts. And, indeed, when prospective associates are given the tour of the workplace, they are shown the amenities first, rather than the production, shipping, and administrative resources that make that very job opportunity possible. Many candidates interviewing for a position are scandalized to hear that cellular phones are not provided or that the company car is a two-year-old economy model. (We suggest that their factory tour be limited to the Exit door.) But self-confident managers, who themselves laugh at the other companies who've "got it soft," will be able to attract employees less concerned with perks and more concerned with belonging to the very best company in the industry.

Just as a taxpayer would be offended if he saw a Marine flying first class while he was scrunched up in coach, customers are taken aback at overt displays of wealth by a company they are dealing with. Most customers, for example, would rather be taken to lunch in a two-year-old economy sedan than in a brand-new Mercedes. They quite naturally do not want to feel that they are contributing to another company's excessive overhead. Even if the customer is unaware of the corporate jet and the lavish executive retreat, the competition will point out such extravagance and present itself as a lean, mean, more cost-effective alternative.

Create Confidence in the Organization

When a Marine is sent into combat, the Marine Corps wants him to have as much confidence as possible—in himself, in his unit, in his leaders, and in the organization as a whole. It has, therefore, refined confidence-building to a science. Recruits come to believe in themselves and in their brother and sister Marines by overcoming the carefully planned challenges of boot camp. Realistic maneuvers follow basic training and continue throughout a Marine's career, creating a sense of unity so strong that communications on the battlefield become almost telepathic. Marines have faith in their leaders because their training is even more difficult and because Marine officers personally display confidence themselves, under even the most dire circumstances. Lastly, Marines have confidence in the 223-year-old Corps itself, and in its terrifying integration of air, sea, and land forces. Of course, it doesn't hurt that America's potential enemies have a mortal fear of the Marines.

Beyond the realm of its own organization, the Marine

Corps creates confidence in the entire national consciousness, through a bombardment of symbols. The President of the United States may fly in Air Force One, but as soon as he is on camera, he is greeted by a saluting Marine. If a shorter trip is required, he boards a Marine Corps helicopter and momentarily waves at the media. The presidential band, which can be seen welcoming dignitaries on the prime-time news, is a Marine Corps band. Every American embassy—the personification of the United States abroad—is guarded by the Marines. The most recognized war memorial of all time—the Iwo Jima flag-raising monument—is so famous that the other services don't even bother to compete with their own memorials in the nation's capital. Slogans like "Send in the Marines" are used in everyday speech fifty years after World War II to indicate the seriousness of a situation. And, when Hollywood makes a war movie, chances are it will involve the Marines. These recurring symbols, coupled with the spectacular record of its success, contribute to the great public faith in the United States Marines Corps.

Corporate management has a very similar need to instill confidence—both throughout its own rank and file and in the minds of its customers and stockholders. Employees who do not believe in their own abilities to represent the company will convince no one of the benefits of its products and services. Without confidence in their team or department, they will give up on assigned goals from the start or attempt to meet them by sacrificing quality or profit. Employees who have no faith in their leaders will try to find shortcuts to success of their own, rather than follow the corporate directive. And, lacking confidence in the organization itself, they will quake in their boots at market rumors, material shortages, or the loss of major customers—sending out resumes instead of joining forces with management to pull the company through. And, of course, an internal lack of confidence will soon manifest itself in the marketplace, frightening off customers and investors alike.

Upper management would be wise to emulate the Marine

Corps' approach to confidence-building. The best "basic" and ongoing training in the industry will make for self-assured employees who can aggressively represent the company or firmly defend it against the claims of a competitor. Faith in one's unit or department can be enhanced with training exercises, regular team meetings to review recent successes or failures and to strategize for the next opportunity, and frequent recognition of the team as a whole. Upper management can help instill trust in itself by communicating its credentials to the rank and file (this is no time for false modesty) and by radiating confidence themselves—worried leaders tend to clone worried subordinates.

Confidence in the organization itself can best be created the Marine Corps way: with internal displays of power (e.g., new product rollouts, factory tours, demonstrations of product superiority), ubiquitous symbols of corporate history (e.g., photographs of the early days of the company, portraits of past leaders, "antique" products displays) and constant communication with the rank and file (about customer feedback, the announcement of major contracts, research and development updates). And remember, confidence flows in both directions; a CEO who is having a bad day can be buoyed by the optimism of his workforce, even though he may be worried sick.

Create Displays of Power

For all its quite necessary secrecy, the military is not averse to showing off. Parades, air shows, and open houses on vast weapon platforms such as nuclear aircraft carriers inspire both the military and civilian populations—not to mention our potential enemies—with a sense of awe. But nobody has a better seat to watch Uncle Sam flex his muscles than the rank-and-file Marine.

Marines have a unique perspective on the application of power because they are in the midst of it, coordinating the air, sea, and ground forces that, together, can turn the best-trained enemy into a panicked mob. A Marine private sees the big picture of integrated force better than many officers in the other services; his training exposes him to all kinds of chaos. Ships, jets, helicopters, landing craft, tanks, and light armored vehicles work in concert with Marines who are on the ground, parachuting out of the sky, and even swimming beneath the waves. The effect of the combined forces is literally staggering, which is another reason why Marines may walk a little taller than their soldier and sailor counterparts.

In private enterprise, there are some employees, as well, who seem to walk a little taller than their counterparts. When Boeing rolled out the 777, the first to see it was their own workforce, during an elaborate and very costly celebration. Thousands of employees attended, eager to see the finished product they all had had a hand in producing. All walked away conscious of their own contributions and, moreover, conscious of the corporate might of Boeing.

But how many employees have never seen their own company's resources proudly displayed? Factory tours, ceremonial product rollouts, and internal self-aggrandizing notices all serve to make each employee, from the person who sweeps the floor to the CEO, aware and proud of his company's strengths. One cannot lead effectively without being proud of the organization one serves.

Avoid the Pitfalls of Personality Worship

Ask any intelligent citizen to name a few famous American military leaders from World War II, and the legendary names of Patton, MacArthur, Eisenhower, Halsey, Nimitz, and LeMay will no doubt be among the first. Conspicuously missing, however, will be the names of even a couple of well-known Marine Corps generals. There are two reasons for this. The Marine Corps, being the smallest of the branches of the armed forces, is rarely "in charge" of a war—at least from the standpoint of the news media. The second reason lies in the nature of the Corps itself.

The strong sense of unity within the Marine Corps does

not lend itself to the creation of highly visible leaders; it seems to have the opposite effect. Generals, after all, come up through the officer ranks, and Marine Corps officers are quick to give all the credit for any successes to the men they command. Marine officers would surely provide dull interviews, thwarting questions that would imply their personal leadership skills were responsible for the victories achieved. In fact, the whole story of the Marine Corps seems to belie the "great man theory" of history, which attributes the turning of events in human affairs to the strong, charismatic leader who steps forward, ahead of all others, and takes charge. When the Marines go down in history, they do it together.

This is why the names of famous Marine generals are not linked, in the mind of the public, to famous Marine Corps victories. We remember MacArthur vowing to return to the Philippines and Patton turning the tide at the Battle of the Bulge, but what Marine generals were responsible for the victories at Iwo Jima and Tarawa? The most famous Marine leaders are virtually unknown outside of the Corps, and that is how they would want it. It is as if they have been too humbled by the sacrifices of their fellow Marines to accept any personal credit. The Marine commandant himself, in his taped speech to graduate recruits, never refers to his own role in the combat examples he shares, although he has a chest-full of medals. Instead, he comes across almost as an awed witness to the bravery of the other Marines around him.

In the world of business, there has long been a journalistic tradition of attributing a company's successes, or failures, to its charismatic leader—from Henry Ford to Bill Gates. Even CEOs of fledgling corporations can find themselves profiled in one of the many new glossy business magazines on the newsstand today. Those who lead larger companies frequently grace the covers of *Business Week*, *Fortune*, and *Forbes* magazines.

This media attention is both personally flattering and, since it is seen as free advertising, complimentary to the company as well. Some corporate leaders hire media coaches to prepare them for the studio interviews they are so eager to attend. Men in their sixties consider facelifts and hair transplants for the first time in their lives in order to present a more dynamic image. Well-known business leaders are hounded by the press, like political figures. Reporters try to elicit provocative comments, as if one word from these gods of industry could trigger a reaction on Wall Street. The big news always seems to be speculation: what dynamic CEO will rescue what floundering corporate giant—as if a new figure atop the flow chart were the only requirement necessary. The magazine photographs themselves seem to underscore the importance of personality. Years ago, in school textbooks and newspapers, businesses were represented with panoramic photos of enormous factories, where armies of men and women labored. Today, close-up portraits of the CEO's face symbolize his company on the covers of business magazines, blotting out all else.

This "great man" theory of business has many pitfalls. Some business leaders, seduced by the media attention, begin to believe their own press. They begin to believe that they—not the organization—are responsible for recent successes in the marketplace. Soon, media considerations intrude into what used to be strictly business decisions; the CEO wonders how his personal marketing may be affected. He may find himself unconsciously resume building while at a public forum or demurring like a politician when asked if he would entertain the thought of leading another corporation.

Meanwhile, the distance between the CEO and the people within his organization widens. Those on the front lines of his company feel they have been denied proper recognition. The free advertising, which once seemed so attractive, is now a source of resentment to the employees who feel left behind by their leader.

Of course, as any politician who has fallen from grace can tell you, a darling of the press can quickly become a scapegoat. Credited personally for the successes of his company, the celebrity CEO may then be blamed exclusively for its failures. And while, as a business leader, he would agree that personal responsibility goes with the territory, he may be unprepared for the cursory analysis by the news media of very complex issues. Since positive character traits were credited for his company's success, it follows, journalistically, that character defects are responsible for its failures (a "loss of nerve," for example, or the reverse—a "reckless abandon").

We are not suggesting a CEO should avoid media opportunities to promote his company; we simply remind him that, like the anonymous Marine Corps general, he might step away from the bright light and let it shine upon the men and women of the organization he has the honor to lead.

Issue a Core Values Card

The Marine Corps has a unique way of reminding its members of their duties to themselves, and to the Corps. Since 1995, a credit-card-size core values card has been issued to every Marine, summarizing, in a few words, the substantial responsibilities inherent in being a member of the world's elite fighting force. On the front are words representing some of the key concepts taught to each Marine in basic training, such as honor, courage, commitment, and integrity; on the back are eight rules of conduct a Marine is expected to follow. Each Marine signs the back of his card, although it is not used for identification purposes. It is meant to be a hip pocket reminder of what a Marine—private or general—stands for.

At first glance, one is surprised that such a card is issued to adults; it seems more appropriate in the wallet of a Boy Scout. None of the other services pass out core values cards, and if they did, it is very possible that there would be some laughter in the rank and file. Why, after all, would a grown man require a card in his wallet to remind him of who he is? Aren't dog tags enough? And, if Marine training is so thorough, and esprit de corps so high, why is the card even necessary? One would think that the Marines would be the last branch of the armed forces that needed a core values card, not the first.

True to tradition, the Marine Corps does not want to leave anything to chance. It may offer the best training in the world, but if that training is not constantly reinforced, it may be forgotten. Recruits leave boot camp, for example, in the best shape of their lives, but muscles have short memories. If full-fledged Marines were not required to excel at quarterly physical fitness tests, they might not be ready for the combat assignment that could come at any moment. Similarly, the hundred or so hours spent on the moral and ethical training of each recruit at boot camp must be reinforced throughout his career.

The Marine core values are not allowed to be floating abstractions; each value is made relevant and personally understandable by interactive sessions. There are discussion groups that make the recruit realize how these core values actually apply to daily life. The lofty principles of honor, courage, and commitment are brought to bear upon issues such as child abuse, suicide, sexual harassment, drug abuse, racism, stealing, and drinking. Recruits are taken through difficult scenarios they are likely to encounter and asked the proper way to deal with them. A recruit might be asked, for example, what he should do if he thought he saw a fellow Marine stealing, or if his buddy told him in confidence that he did not like living and working with members of a particular race. The drill instructor, for once speaking in a quiet voice, will guide the recruit through his thinking until he discovers, for himself, the proper answer.

Core value cards are not put in the wallet and forgotten. A Marine's superior may ask him, out of the blue, to name one of the core values. Not content with a memorized reiteration, the officer may ask him to explain, in his own words, what the core value means to him personally. This is one way the Marine Corps hopes to make the great lessons learned in boot camp unforgettable.

It is interesting to note that nobody laughs at the Core Value Card. "If I ever heard one of my men snicker," says Staff Sergeant John LaMantia, "I'd take him aside and ask him 'Which core value do you think is so funny—honor, courage, or commitment?' And I'd be very interested to hear his answer."

Companies, too, have core values. Immediately after a new employee's indoctrination period, he probably would have no difficulty reiterating them. A year or so later, however, he might be hard pressed to name even one. A company core values card is certainly one of the easiest ways to reinforce the fundamental concepts learned during "basic training."

As in the Marine version, key words on the front of the card can represent the corporate vision; on the back, the company's expectations of the employee could be spelled out. Like Marines, each associate can sign the card, thereby acknowledging the standards by which he must abide. If the company already uses some form of card for employee identification or access control, the solution is even easier: simply preprint the core values on the back.

A core values card would serve the same purpose for the company as it does for the Marine Corps, and more, since they could also be used for advertising. Business cards, for example, could be printed with the core values for all the world to see. Customers may be so impressed that they will begin issuing core values cards themselves—a form of flattery that would further solidify the existing relationship.

The corporate core values could appear at the top of company letterheads and on invoices, postage meter indicia, paychecks, visitor badges, and virtually any form of communication to employees, customers, vendors, and the general public. Whatever the means used, the key to the credibility of the message would be, of course, the behavior of each member of the organization. We would hope that the words on the core values card represent more than just words.

Create Loyalty

The life of a Marine is not an easy one at any point during his career. Yet, the loyalty of Marines—to each other, to their superiors, and to the Corps itself—is legendary. Its very motto—Semper Fidelis (Always Faithful)—is an indication of how much value the Corps places upon the virtue of loyalty. This sense of fidelity does not come from simply taking an oath; young recruits barely out of their teens who pledge to defend the Constitution are, at that moment, uttering words they have not yet learned the meaning of. Loyalty is not demanded by the Marine Corps; it is created, on both an institutional level and a personal one.

Institutionally, the Marine Corps first sets the conditions in which a close affiliation will form. Its recruiting message— "Do you have what it takes to be one of us?"—attracts a certain kind of individual, one who would be likely to value membership in the Corps. Its rite of passage—boot camp—creates a sense of mutual trust; each Marine knows that everyone who wears the uniform has what it takes to endure those twelve unforgettable weeks. The constant maneuvers in which Marines participate throughout their hitch forge a team spirit they are literally willing to die for. Combat veterans confirm time and again that, when the chips are down, "Marines fight for each other." (*Fleet Marine Force Manual* 1–0)

The sense of belonging is further cemented by the official and unofficial actions of the officers and noncommissioned officers, who have been trained to consider the welfare of their men before their own. These leaders ask a lot of their Marines but give a lot in return. The Hollywood version of the Marine Corps, where officers and sergeants bark orders at intimidated men, would hardly be, in reality, an environment distinguished by loyalty. Loyalty is freely given; it cannot be coerced. Most Marines will go the extra mile for their squad leaders or platoon commanders because these leaders have gone the extra mile for them; it's that simple.

Loyalty in private enterprise is a great concern to managers at all levels. There is a very real need for confidentiality—to protect proprietary information such as pricing, product development, and customer lists—but no mechanism to enforce it, other than termination and perhaps prosecution after the damage has been done. Employees may sign pieces of paper, promising not to work for the competition for one year after leaving the corporation, but every "sea lawyer" in the company knows these agreements do not hold up in court; a person cannot be deprived of his means to make a living. Loyalty oaths are no longer allowed (as if loyalty could ever be compelled). A company's best employees are courted by the competition all the time; and when they suddenly leave, there are many sleepless nights in upper management. Not only can an exiting manager, for example, take valuable information with him; he can take half his department along with him as well—an example of loyalty on the personal level, but not on the institutional.

Internal criminal theft is another major concern in businesses today. Retail stores lose more merchandise through employee theft than through shoplifting customers. Camera systems must be installed to monitor employees who undercharge their friends at the counter or walk away from warehouse loading docks with company goods. Personal purchases are "expensed" by cynical employees, who feel the company can afford it. While these are all examples of basic dishonesty, such abuses would rarely occur in an environment that elicited loyalty from its employees.

Loyalty can be created in free enterprise—if the company and its managers do it the Marine Corps way. The company must first set the conditions in which a mixture of pride and gratitude for just belonging can be established. The standards for employment should be high; the training should be the best. Even if the amenities are not commensurate with similar companies in the industry (Marines have the most Spartan facilities and yet the highest morale), employees should feel as if they are working for the best company in the business, bar none. The team concept should be implemented throughout the rank and file of the company; remember: Marines fight for each other. And if cost cutting is ever required, let the employees see the corporate jet sold before any layoffs are ordered; the executives can fly coach.

On the front lines, the manager has only to look out for

the welfare of his own personnel with the same attention given by a Marine officer or sergeant to experience similar expressions of loyalty. An employee who has been helped during an emergency, or publicly recognized for his performance, or protected because of a mistake, or emotionally supported during a difficult time will never forget it. When the competition's headhunter calls with a job offer, he will feel as if he is being asked to leave his family. When the temptation to fudge on his expense report arises, he will remember the decency of his manager and tear up the receipt. And when he is asked to stay late to help his boss make a deadline, he will be grateful for the opportunity to repay a debt.

Handle Scandals Personally

Despite its disciplined way of life, the military is not exempt from internal problems. At the time of this writing, every branch of the armed forces was either in the news or had been recently because of an internal scandal. The navy had to deal with the well-publicized accusations of sexual harassment in the Tailhook incident. A woman air force pilot's romance became a media saga during her discharge proceedings for adultery. The highest ranking enlisted man in the army, its sergeant major, was prominently in the news, denying multiple accusations of sexual harassment. And the Marine Corps had to deal with a shocking crime in Okinawa, where two Marines had confessed to raping a young girl.

All of these stories had long "shelf lives" in the media, appearing again and again on our television screens and in print—all, that is, except for the worst offense of them all, the actions of the two Marines. That story was short-lived, primarily, we believe, because of the courageous leadership of the Commandant of the Marine Corps. Rather than sitting behind closed office doors, delegating the official responses to Pentagon spokespeople, General Krulak immediately went to Okinawa. He faced the local community representatives and expressed his disgust for the crime, as well as the sympathies of a father to the young girl and her family. He then, in seventeen hours, visited the seven Marine Corps bases on Okinawa and spoke to more than 21,000 Marines. "I wanted to tell them that their commandant loves them and that the Marine Corps has not lost faith in them," he said. Perhaps unwittingly, General Krulak completely disarmed the news media. What tough questions could the reporters possibly ask of a man who did not try to obfuscate the truth and who, at the same time, remained completely devoted to his organization? The two offenders were sentenced by the local authorities and that was the end of the story.

Every CEO who reads this should remember that the commandant was acting out of love for his Corps, not out of concerns for damage control. In fact, if he *had* tried to control the damage, the news media would have had a field day with him (as it did with the other service scandals). But by acting out of love, and by personally exemplifying the honesty and courage America expects from its Marines, he put this tragic incident into perspective. The Marine Corps emerged from a potential public relations disaster with its reputation unsullied.

CEOs who boldly step forward to face the media to acknowledge the seriousness of a situation, to express their own heart-felt concern for the injured parties, and to openly express their confidence and pride in the organization they lead will win the respect of customers, investors, and employees alike. The public wants to know that someone is in charge of the company, that he earnestly wants to find out what went wrong, and that it will not be business as usual until he does. And the employees, like the 21,000 Marines in Okinawa, who were bearing the brunt of local ill will for the actions of two, want to know that their boss still stands by them. A public relations team cannot accomplish any of this; it takes a leader.

Throw a Birthday Party!

Each November 10, all over the world—in formal toasts or in solitary raisings of a glass to the images of lost comrades—

Marines and former Marines alike salute the birthday of their Corps. No military celebration is as well known as the birthday of the United States Marine Corps. Although the average citizen might be hard pressed to come up with the actual date, it occurs to him as a kind of afterthought, an "ah, yes, it's their birthday," as Marines in dress blues seem to appear everywhere—at football games, shopping malls, high school campuses, and Main Street parades. Images of Marines cutting the birthday cake are on the televised news and in the papers. Any Madison Avenue guru would agree: the Marine Corps birthday is a tremendous public relations achievement. For a very little investment, the Marines have an unparalleled opportunity to boost internal morale, endear themselves to the American public, spike recruiting all over the nation, and send a signal abroad—to potential enemies—that the Corps is alive and well and ready for anything.

This media attention, of course, does not happen without an aggressive campaign on the part of the Marine Corps, which contacts every conceivable publicity outlet. The Marine Corps birthday is a global news item—not because the press marks it on their calendars but because the Marines make such a big deal about it, so big, in fact, that the army, navy, and air force, which certainly must also have birthdays, do not even attempt to compete. The Marine Corps has cornered the market on birthdays.

It is interesting, too, that the celebration is a birthday, rather than an anniversary of the day the Marine Corps was formed in 1775. Birthdays are for living entities; anniversaries are to commemorate what has happened, not what is happening. Birthdays are a time for celebration; anniversaries a time for reflection. Birthdays are a time for giving gifts (in the case of the Marine Corps, continued taxpayer support); anniversaries are a time for the laying of wreaths. And the Marine Corps, the smallest and least funded branch of the armed forces, is much more interested in gifts.

It is incredible that so few companies celebrate their birthdays. Whether the company is young or old, there are very compelling reasons for upper management to throw an annual birthday bash. It is a terrific PR opportunity, raising morale within the company, and customer awareness without.

Internally, employees are reminded of the company's stability, but also of its mortality; a birthday party reinforces the desire to protect and to perpetuate. A time for festivities, it is also a time for sentimentality. Everyone should be reminded that the company's well-being depends upon their continued support and performance and that their own well-being is connected to that of the flourishing company.

Externally, assuming the PR department does its job, customers are reminded of the existence of the company, of its longevity—and of the validity of its "lifetime" warranty. But even a very young business profits from the customer's awareness. There is something about a company's one-year birthday party, earnestly celebrated, that makes one want to wish it the best. The community, too, is reminded through press releases and ads, of the company's contribution in taxes and jobs and charitable support.

An annual birthday party doesn't have to cost a lot; potluck affairs or wine and cheese parties will have the same positive effects as gala balls. Upper management has no reason not to exploit, and to enjoy, this recurring opportunity to the fullest—with press releases, advertisements, speeches, ceremony, and plenty of festivities.

Stick With Core Expertise

The Marine Corps is a very confident organization. And there must be times, after a particularly successful maneuver or rescue mission, when the Marines in the rank and file feel as if they could take on the world. But their generals know better. Being the smallest branch of the service helps keep things in perspective. The Marine Corps may be a legendary fighting machine, but its role is limited. While Marines are generally the "first to fight," they may not be around for the victory celebrations.

The Marine Corps is most effective when used as the nation's 911 force. It trains to get in quickly, and then to get out. The Marine Corps was never intended to remain as an occupational force, nor was it designed to wage war in the conventional sense, on vast battlefields where huge armies and thousands of tanks contend. During the Cold War, when Pentagon planners developed scenarios in which western Europe opposed a Soviet land invasion, the U.S. Army played the major role, because that's what it was designed to do. Marine generals do not feel slighted by playing second fiddle in conventional exercises, or even in actual confrontations, such as Desert Storm, which was a textbook example of why the nation also needs an army.

Marine Corps generals never forget their core expertise. While it has jet fighters, the Marine Corps will never be an air force; and, despite its many tanks, it is not the army. On Capitol Hill, and in meetings with the Joint Chiefs of Staff, Marine generals protect the Corps from being assigned inappropriate missions. On the other hand, they positively demand commands of the kinds of missions that the Marines have refined to an art form, such as amphibious assaults, rescue operations, behind-the-lines infiltration—and any operation requiring a rapid seaborne response. Once "the Marines have landed," the larger branches of the armed forces have time to amass their considerable power. And, once the army moves in—to keep the peace—the Marines are sent back to their ships to prepare for the next emergency.

When it comes to "growing the business," CEOs are often damned if they do and damned if they don't. Those who fail to increase market share are not considered aggressive; those who pioneer uncharted territory, and get lost, are accused of straying away from the company's core expertise. There are many chief executive officers who, having leaped into a new marketplace, now wish they had walked—or even crawled—instead.

A veteran business leader is in no hurry to venture from an established market. His marketing people may speak of a "mature" market—one that has already peaked and now grows at a sedate 1 or 2 percent—but that doesn't mean his business cannot grow at a faster rate. By sticking with its core expertise, the company's reputation continues to grow, and it is recognized as a leader in its industry. Eventually, its competitors, persuaded by the talk of mature markets, may abandon the industry altogether, leaving the company with more opportunities, with less competition, in a business it knows inside and out.

There are very few, if any, true monopolies in America. No matter how successful a corporation becomes, it has competitors. And as long as rivals are knocking on the doors of his existing and potential customers, the CEO has a job to finish in that mature market—and that is to run his competitors out of town.

But "sticking to his guns" does not mean that a CEO should never venture into new territory. Even Marine Corps generals take on missions for which the Marines were not designed; but they ask Congress for the necessary resources to carry that mission out. Similarly, the veteran CEO is careful not to outpace his own ability to support an undertaking into a new industry, or a vastly different territory.

The Marine Corps didn't build its legendary reputation by trying amphibious landings in one battle, round-the-clock air raids in another, and massive tank invasions in yet another. It stayed within its expertise and literally wrote the book on the science of amphibious landings. Today, after "hitting the beach" no fewer than three hundred times in actual combat, it is the recognized master of the seaborne assault. The Marines have mastered other forms of warfare, as well—such as helicopter and paratroop attack and antiterrorist strikes—but these are logical extensions of their core expertise. CEOs on the verge of leaping into an unfamiliar industry or territory would do well to keep the example of the Corps in mind and build upon their own competency.

See for Yourself

Marine Corps generals in a combat operation have at their disposal decision-making resources so advanced as to border on the omniscient. Vital information on the enemy's disposition simply pours in—from satellites, high-altitude reconnaissance flights, Marine "force recon" intelligence units behind the lines, computerized topographical software systems, and sophisticated electronic eavesdropping devices. Why, then, do the generals insist—sometimes against vehement protests from the Pentagon—on climbing into a helicopter to go see the battleground for themselves?

We have to remember that these generals were once lieutenants, and Marine Corps officers are trained to command from a forward position. They have learned from personal experience, in combat and in maneuver, that state-of-the-art intelligence technologies do not tell the whole story. Topographical maps, for example, can detail the rise in ground elevation to the inch but say nothing of the kinds of vegetation that can make even a moderate slope impenetrable. Intelligence reports on enemy positions do not indicate how determined they are to resist. And the morale of one's own Marines can best be determined by a personal visit. If their spirits happen to be low, they will be buoyed by the presence of the general, who has had the courage to share the risk.

By seeing for himself, the general can get a better idea of how his officers have deployed their forces. In fact, his very presence is a tacit acknowledgment and approval of that deployment, which affiliates the high command with the decentralized decisions made in the field. In case of an inquiry later, the general has voluntarily placed himself in the hot seat, alongside his officers. And, finally, there are subtle, intuitive insights to be gained from a personal visit to the front; the older veteran may recognize certain alignments of forces or land formations that trigger a red flag, reminding him of hard-learned lessons from years ago.

CEOs are under a similar obligation to frequently visit the "front lines." Veteran business leaders know from experience that in-house and outsourced information, while useful, does not tell the whole story. For one thing, reports can be biased by personality; a pessimist and an optimist may have very different interpretations of how a major project is faring or different evaluations of a business opportunity. Even unbiased messages can be innocently misconstrued in passage. And, despite his orders to the contrary, his subordinates will be tempted to tell the boss what they think he wants to hear. Like the general, the CEO must go see for himself.

It is important, however, that a visit from the top not be seen by the rank and file as a sign of distrust. Marine generals do not visit the battle area because they mistrust their officers; they go because they owe it to themselves, and to the Corps, to give the benefit of their experience to the evaluation of the situation. While at the job site, or the customer's office—or wherever the front lines happen to be—the CEO should openly endorse his managers so that there is no suggestion of a loss of confidence. He is there only to support his people and to share the wisdom of a lifetime in business. The CEO is, after all, the ultimate mentor; every opportunity to pass on a legacy of experience should be taken.

A visit to the front lines also gives the CEO a chance to see the occasional star performer who might never otherwise have been brought to his attention. He will be able to see for himself if more resources should be thrown into the project. Very often subordinates deny the need for more corporate support—not out of fear of appearing to falter but out of a proud confidence in their own hard-working personnel. Sometimes a CEO has to force a brave manager to accept help, by making it clear that his success will only be accelerated, not diminished. A trip to the front will also help him assess the needs of his customers; he may find the customer feedback—unfiltered by Sales or Service—to be very enlightening. And there should, of course, be periodic visits to the "rear," as well—to the factory floor or warehouse—so that he can see for himself the condition of the infrastructure and the safety of the work-ing conditions. Lunch at the employee cafeteria will give him a chance to simultaneously boost morale and listen to some of the concerns of the workforce.

A general's visit to the front lines is usually a surprise; he doesn't want resources to be diverted for his personal safety, and he hopes to catch the environment as it is, without the benefit of preparation for a visit from the top brass. The CEO of a business has fewer concerns with safety, we hope, but he too should appear without notice, or with very little notice, for the same reason. Of course, once the boss arrives, things will be a little different. His presence will heighten the per-formance of those around him. Conversely, his own perform-ance will be enhanced by the opportunity to be of service to his employees.

Prevent Workplace Violence

Years ago it was unheard of for an employee to go on a shooting rampage at his place of work; today it is almost a common occurrence. Chief executive officers, motivated by concern for their employees—not to mention the fear of litigation for not having taken precautions against "foreseeable" workplace vio-lence—now spend billions of dollars annually on security sys-tems and procedures designed to protect employees, and themselves for that matter, from harm while on the job.

It is interesting that the Marine Corps spends very little on internal security systems—in an environment where every-body is armed to the teeth! There are so few incidents of work-place violence that it is almost unheard of. This is no accident, however, it is a consequence of enlightened leadership.

Due to its constant obsession for combat readiness, Ma-rine Corps life is stressful for the rank and file and for officers. There must be times when individuals are tempted to lash out at each other. But the day-to-day working culture of the Ma-rine Corps is not a permissive one. When one reads newspaper profiles of employees who have gone berserk, it always seems that they have a history of smaller incidents of violence on the job, each one more serious than the previous. It would be very difficult for a Marine to exhibit progressively negative behavior; in fact he wouldn't get to first base. His peers, his superiors, his entire world would be intolerant of the first, even trivial, offense; if such an incident happened, it would stop there. The Marine Corps has created an environment that enforces respect for others. Temper tantrums and threats are not, by common consensus, allowed to occur, much less repeated. Marines would be shocked to hear what angry employees get away with at their jobs; they would wonder what is wrong with the leadership in private enterprise.

We are not suggesting that a stern, no-nonsense mandate from the top makes for an obedient workplace. Marines are happy people; life on a base is robust, and even has its share of nonsense. But the expectation of each Marine is that he will be treated fairly, by everyone who wears the uniform. That standard has been set, and exemplified, by the Corps' commandant and by every one of his predecessors.

Marines have been told from Day One that they are something special—not because they wear the uniform, but because they work so hard to be worthy of the uniform. That kind of self-esteem, and mutual respect does not breed workplace violence. And since each Marine is a part a team, personal dissatisfaction and anger—if they do occur—dissipate very quickly through the counseling of team members. And the instant an officer senses disharmony in the ranks, correcting it becomes his highest priority. He and his sergeant discover the problem and do whatever it takes to resolve it—not by barking orders but through personal and compassionate intervention.

In private enterprise, security of the workplace is no less a leadership issue, and nobody can do more to ensure a safe working environment than the chief executive officer. It is the CEO who sets the tone of the workplace and who creates an environment of self-esteem, mutual respect, and zero tolerance for any form of abuse—from the top down, or peer to peer. Rather than delegating the concern for workplace harmony to his human resources or security director, he places it in the hands of the team members throughout the rank and file of the entire organization. Open himself, he instructs his managers to be solicitous of their subordinates, approachable, and proactive. By personal example and mandate, he creates a corporate culture much like that in the Marine Corps, in which the welfare of the individual is paramount and in which team members care for each other. Such an environment is not fertile ground for workplace violence.

Start a CEO's Suggested Reading List

At any Marine Corps base store, the visitor will find just about everything a well-stocked convenience store would carry. There is one display, however, that is unique. In a prominent location, there will be a few shelves of books—away from the paperbacks and magazines section. A sign hanging over it from the ceiling reads COMMANDANT'S READING LIST.

One will find on the shelves below works of military history (not all of them having to do with the Marine Corps), books on leadership and strategy, biographies, and novels. There will be a title list, with an indication of which books are suggested for officers, which for noncommissioned officers, and which for the rank and file. This segregation is not meant to be pretentious; it is, rather a guide, although obviously any individual can purchase any book he chooses. It also lets the subordinate know what kinds of material he should be concerned with at the next rank.

Of course, this is only a suggested reading list, but it's not surprising that, given the source, a great many Marines buy—and then read—these books. While there is no official mechanism for monitoring the program, there are subtle pressures that encourage participation. A sergeant, for example, may ask one of his Marines about a scene in C. S Forester's *Rifleman Dodd* (which, at the time of this writing, is on the list); if the young man hasn't read the novel, he gets the distinct impression he had better. Of course, the sergeant is getting the same treatment from *his* superior officer, who in turn wants to be conversant with the topics his superior is reading, and so on.

The books on the list have been picked by the commandant for a reason: each one, in its own way, reinforces the great lessons taught by the Marine Corps. History, biography, or fiction, the books are another way of keeping the message of honor, courage, and commitment alive. Politically, the list is neutral; Marines must, after all, serve every president, Democratic, Republican, or third-party. But the books chosen do have a definite bias. The commandant is not about to recommend books that in any way contradict the lessons the Marine Corps has worked so hard to pass on. Unlike a college administrator, the commandant is under no obligation to offer equal time to opposing views; one won't find *Das Kapital* or *Mein Kampf* on the reading list.

Since this is not a compulsory program, the commandant really has no accurate way of knowing how many of his Marines actually read, much less enjoy, these books. Sales figures are not an accurate reference, because the books tend to be passed around when finished. But, from anecdotal experience, the number seems to be high. Certainly, it is a lot higher than it would be without the program.

Why can't a CEO put out his own suggested reading list to reinforce the corporate vision and core values? An attractive display at every employee lounge of books to be freely borrowed, or purchased, will generate interest and participation. Of course, the program has to be purely voluntary, but many employees will wish to be conversant with the material others are talking about. Those who wanted to make an impression on their managers will initiate the conversations—as the managers themselves will do with their own superiors. The books will be another point of contact between individuals, who might find themselves conversing on topics other than the weekend football games.

By simply distributing the list and displaying the books prominently, the CEO will set into motion a chain of events that can greatly benefit the workplace. Very simply, his employees may read more. A number of things may happen, all of them good. His employees may become interested in the reading materials and become more interesting, themselves. Reading thought-provoking books may open their minds to thinking "out of the box" at work; they may begin to occasionally think of themselves in the third person, as a fictional character, and begin to plan their careers in earnest. Impromptu discussions will no doubt take place in the lunch rooms and employee lounges, in which the merits of the CEO's picks are considered.

Of course the suggested reading list must be of an apolitical, work-specific nature, but that leaves open an enormous selection of inspirational and informative material. The CEO must choose carefully; the books must reinforce the Corporate Way and not his own particular values, unless they happen to coincide. But certainly books on leadership, organizational skills, time management, business strategies, sales strategies, public speaking, biographies, market trends, and company histories can be suggested without fear of offending any employee. Since the program is optional and not monitored, no one will feel oppressed or obligated to participate. But, for a very cost-effective investment, management will have yet another way to strengthen the corporate message.

Yes Sir, No Sir

A Marine is taught to punctuate every thought or reply with a "Sir!" For the first twelve weeks of boot camp, he must even begin each sentence to a superior with a "Sir!" Young men who may have come from tough neighborhoods or families in which deference to another was considered a display of weakness are now "sir-ing" and saluting everybody they meet. The civilian visitor to a Marine base, who is accustomed to being treated indifferently, at best, by others, is at once startled and gratified by the courtesy of the men and women in Marine uniforms. He will never be called "Sir" so many times again, unless he revisits the base. And, driving away, he feels a little more important—and a little more protected—than he did upon arriving.

The Marine's courtesy is not an affectation. It may be habitual, but the habit is born of a curious mixture of humility and self-respect and an ingrained desire to be of service to somebody. The humility comes from being torn down by his drill instructors, the self-respect from being subsequently built up, and the eagerness to serve others from the occasional grin of the D.I. when he did something right. Boot camp is not charm school, but the recruit who graduates is often unrecognizable to his parents and friends, who haven't seen him for three months. The loud-mouthed, wise-cracking adolescent who ran off to join the Marines now speaks to his parents in a way that would have embarrassed him before basic training. The "Sirs" and "Ma'ams" abound. He stands when they stand. Even his language has been cleaned up; there was more cursing in high school than he has heard in boot camp.

How often do we leave a retail store, or a customer service counter, disgusted with the apathetic and even downright rude behavior of a company representative? It is one of the great ironies of modern business that, as customer service becomes the differentiating factor between one company and its increasingly numerous competitors, common courtesy from employees seems to be on the decline. If there was ever a need for service with a smile, it is now. In so many industries, the customer can buy the identical commodity off the shelves at any number of stores, companies, or factories. Price being fairly equal, the comparative service of the competing outlets is the only possible remaining factor to consider in deciding where to buy.

Yet so many employees who deal with the public do not seem to realize that the only reason left for the customer to buy their product or service is how well he is personally treated. It is not hyperbole to suggest that the very existence of many companies hangs not on the decisions of their visionary CEOs and energetic managers but on the behavior of its receptionists, retail clerks, delivery drivers, and service personnel. If the customer can pick and choose from a number of sources, why would he tolerate indifference, or insolence, from one vendor when there are so many?

If a manager has not called his own customer service desk in a week, then he has no idea how many times the phone will ring before it is answered, how politely the customer will be greeted, how willingly that customer will be helped and then thanked. If that manager has not included customer satisfaction "report cards" with every purchase, installation, or service call, he hasn't the foggiest notion of how well his precious customers are being treated. He must make it perfectly clear to his employees that their jobs depend upon satisfied customers and that customer satisfaction really has less to do with the performance of the product itself than with a customer's unhurried, pleasant interaction with whomever represents the company. Any problem can be overcome by a courteous representative who truly wants to serve the customer.

Employees who consider the customer an intrusion on their time are ubiquitous. Managers in every company would be wise to instill in all of their subordinates some of the courtesy found in the Marines. And it can certainly begin with a lot of "Yes Sirs" and "Yes Ma'ams."

When You Are Gone . . .

While every chief executive officer—of the Marine Corps or of a corporation—gives a thought now and then to the legacy he will leave behind, we believe the general's view of a successful tenure might come as a surprise to the CEO. The general's best confirmation of a truly successful command would be that the Marine Corps went on to function even more effectively under his successors.

We are not suggesting that the general is a selfless, saintly guardian, unconcerned with having a personal impact on the Marine Corps. He certainly does want to leave his mark—but in the hearts and minds of the officers and rank and file around him. And that was the attitude of his predecessor, who groomed him for the job. While a former CEO might be gratified to hear that the company never fared better than under his tenure, the general would be heartbroken; he would consider it a failure of leadership if he did not leave the Marine Corps in better hands than his own.

Of course, the comparison is slightly unfair. CEOs often have not been with their companies as long as many of the employees, while the general has served the Marine Corps for thirty years and is definitely "senior" in every sense of the word. The CEO is sometimes brought in from the outside to "rescue" the company; the general is promoted from within—and nobody has ever had to "rescue" the Marine Corps. The CEO may be selected by search firms contracted by the board of directors; the general is selected by other, more senior generals. The CEO usually works for a company that wasn't around when he was born; the general works for a long-lived organization, one that is more than two hundred years old and counting. The CEO serves the stockholders; the Marine Corps general serves a brotherhood.

But certainly every company would benefit if its CEO considered his legacy to be more important than his reputation. If, like the general, he were to see his responsibilities as a sacred trust, the preparation of the company's future leaders would become the highest priority. This is easier said than done, however. CEOs are measured by increases in profit and market share; there is no space on the balance sheet reserved for "mentoring," nor is there any guarantee that his successor will even come from within the organization. Yet, if the company is to endure, the CEO must strive to bring those around him up to, and beyond, his own capacity. His greatest contribution to the organization he serves should be the quality of the leadership that takes his place.

Leadership Strategies Checklist

—Recognize, and tout, the company's contribution toward a better world.

—Understand that small can be good.

—Apply a "no-frills" culture across the board, and it will be accepted by the employees.

—Instill confidence in the organization—in the employee, the stockholder, and the customer.

—Display corporate power for the benefit of the workplace.

—Discourage "personality worship."

—Issue a corporate Core Values Card.

—Recognize that loyalty is a matter of reciprocity.

—Respond to scandals immediately and forthrightly.

—Celebrate the company's "birthday."

—Don't stray from the company's "core expertise."

—Visit the "front lines" often.

—Understand that preventing workplace violence is a leadership issue, from the top down.

—Implement a "CEO's Reading List."

—Instill a strong habit of courtesy throughout the organization.

—Strive to leave the organization in better hands than your own.

6

A Few Good Women

"When I joined the Marine Corps in 1967, I did so because it offered me an opportunity to earn the respect of people in a superb organization, equal pay for equal work, and a way to learn about the world—by seeing it. That was also the year that the Women's Armed Forces Service Integration Act . . . was amended to allow women the opportunity to be promoted to the rank of General. Little did I know then the implications that change in statute held for me."

—Lieutenant General Carol A. Mutter, Deputy Chief of Staff for Manpower and Reserve Affairs, Headquarters, Marine Corps

"As a woman Marine officer, I never let my gender play into my role as a leader. I found that if I ignored the fact that I was a woman, my Marines would learn to ignore it as well."

—Millie Wilkerson, Vice President/Area Sales Manager of twenty-four branches, Wachovia Bank, former Captain, USMC

When we told the Marines we interviewed that we intended to devote a chapter to women Marines, the response from men and women alike was, "Why a special chapter? The Marine

Corps doesn't treat its women any differently; why should you?"

Well, because the business world does. Despite all the progress that has been made over the years, the corporate environment is still pretty much of a man's world. In many companies, the woman manager or executive earns less money than her male peers, must still contend with an old boys' network, and must disengage herself from the protective, but patronizing, arm around her shoulders from upper management. We believe women who work in male-dominated companies can learn a lot from their female counterparts who have been trained to successfully deal with the most masculine environment of them all—the Marine Corps.

It is difficult to think of another organizational culture that is more of a man's world. The very term "Marine" evokes images of cigar-chewing, tough-talking sergeants, drill instructors from hell, and seemingly suicidal charges into hails of bullets. The Marine Corps' mascot is the pugnacious-looking bulldog (don't tell anybody, but bulldogs are the sweetest of breeds); the Marine-to-Marine greeting is a guttural "OO-RAH!" that, to the uninitiated, sounds more like a growl. Yet, in this most masculine of environments, the orders of female Marine leaders are followed without a thought to their gender. How this happens will be of great interest to every businesswoman.

It should be noted that this chapter is necessarily brief, because, as we noted at the beginning of this book, every leadership principle discussed in this book applies to women Marines as well as to men.

The Leader Within

There is only one Marine boot camp experience, and it is indifferent to gender—everyone is pushed to the limit. Women recruits have drill instructors shouting into their faces, just like the men; they get just as dirty and just as tired. It's definitely no place for a woman.

That is why, from Day One of basic training, the woman recruit is taught to think of herself not as a woman but as a Marine. Boot camp denies the female recruit the very accoutrements the outside culture forces upon her. Just as the male recruit must forgo hair, jewelry, and athletically cut clothes, the woman is reduced to the same common denominator. Although she has tried to prepare herself psychologically for the stresses of boot camp, it still comes as a shock. Makeup and perfume become things of the past. Hair is shorn, stylish clothes are sent back home in a cardboard box like the personal effects of someone who has died. Even her glasses, if she wears them, are replaced by bulky Marine Corps-issue "goggles." She must wear blocky "utilities," which make overalls look fashionable, combat boots, and a heavy steel helmet that keeps sliding down her face. Looking in the mirror—after years of looking in mirrors, dressed presentably for school, or work, or for a date—she now sees an unattractive, frightened stranger.

If she is tempted to feel sorry for herself, she finds no sympathy from her superiors. Whatever ordeal the men recruits are put through, she must also endure. If she cries, she is scorned instead of comforted. During the first few weeks of boot camp, it probably never occurs to her that she will eventually be the equal of any Marine on base, man or woman, and that one day she will be giving orders to many of them.

Marine Corps basic training is really the antithesis of our cultural indoctrination. The efforts of conscientious parents and teachers not withstanding, far too many little girls grow up in America believing that brains and ability are of less importance than personal appeal. Madison Avenue, with its never ending multimedia bombardment, would have women believe that what they wear is more important than what is within. The Marine Corps takes away any such dependencies and forces the woman recruit, and the man, to rely upon a much more substantial foundation of self-esteem and demonstrated competency. Upon graduation, both sexes are allowed to grow their hair back, although it will remain fairly short. Woman Marines will be able to use cosmetics again, and the men will splash on cologne, but both will know that these accessories have nothing whatsoever to do with leadership.

Many women in our society insist that they want to be judged for their ability alone and not their attractiveness, but few take this desire as far as the woman Marine. Most Marines would be surprised to hear the Corps described as a feminist utopia, but there are few environments more blind to gender. A woman Marine has no problem taking orders from, or giving them to, another Marine. Rank is the final arbiter, not gender. The woman in uniform, like the man, is treated simply as a Marine. And that is one reason why the retention rate in the Marine Corps is the same for women and men—about 88 percent.

We are not suggesting that the newly hired female trainees of the corporation report to work with shaved heads and without makeup. We do suggest, however, that both sexes within the corporation may have something to learn from the Marine Corps' insistence that what you put on has nothing to do with your ability to lead. In the image-conscious workplace, men color their hair or glue on expensive (and, sometimes, not so expensive) toupees, wear lifts in their shoes, and undergo cosmetic surgery. And too many women feel equally uncomfortable about themselves. Even an adult woman business executive will occasionally catch herself preoccupied with a distracting hairstyle or facial blemish before a meeting. Both genders would do well to remember Marine recruits, who are purposely "made ugly" during the twelve-week ordeal of boot camp, in order to become confident, self-reliant individuals—on their own, without any assistance from Madison Avenue.

Dealing With Sexual Harassment

The prosecution of sexual harassment in the workplace is a comparatively recent phenomenon. Even in an enlightened society like ours, which has endeavored to protect the rights of the individual, the male prerogative has been so deeply ingrained that—minus a physical attack—many Americans have had difficulty even recognizing what constitutes sexual harassment. Some of the most conscientious men, ready to leap to the defense of every victim of persecution, might be surprised to learn that their behavior toward women—which is very often the behavior of a lifetime—borders on harassment. Our culture seems to have long considered certain kinds of male conduct—from pulling pigtails in a grade-school classroom to making passes at the "girls" at the office—to be inevitable, as if the expression "boys will be boys" described a genetically determined pattern of behavior that could not be modified. The protestations of the woman were not taken seriously by men, who had the audacity to believe that their victims secretly enjoyed such attention. Even the earnest efforts of the feminist movement did not seem to awaken the male consciousness at the workplace. What finally *did* get the attention of at least the corporate leadership was the millions of dollars awarded over recent years to the victims of sexual harassment.

While the armed forces are somewhat more insulated from lawsuits, the repercussions of scandal and accusation can have a severe impact on the retention of existing personnel and the recruitment of new. Careers have been ended; and no one is immune from the process that follows a sexual harassment complaint—not the general, not the commandant, not the commander in chief. Every branch of the service takes the problem very seriously; but only one has been disproportionately successful in dealing with it.

The Marine Corps deals with the issue of sexual harassment by first acknowledging the very real likelihood of its happening. Young men and women generally enlist in the Corps at their sexual peak, around eighteen or twenty years old. They are away from home, perhaps for the first time in their lives. They are under tremendous stress during boot camp, and in great need of emotional support. It would be the most natural thing in the world for a man or woman recruit to seek out a member of the opposite sex. Recognizing this very real possibility, the Marine Corps makes it impossible. Today, it remains the only branch of the armed forces that still segregates its male and female recruits throughout basic training—a practice the more "progressive" services, plagued by scandal and numerous charges of sexual harassment, are now considering reestablishing.

So, for the first twelve weeks of boot camp, the opportunities for any interaction at all between the sexes are denied. During this period, both genders are trained to protect themselves from, and to prevent themselves from committing, acts of sexual harassment.

It might strike the visitor to boot camp as rather incongruous to hear a D.I. lecturing his men recruits on the evils of sexual harassment, but this kind of social awareness is considered vital to the goal of achieving mission readiness. These lectures are definitely not delivered with a wink and a nod; the last thing a drill instructor wants is his beloved Marine Corps on the front page of the newspapers because of a scandal. Nor are they the kinds of talks through which a recruit can daydream. D.I.s have a way of commanding the utmost attention. At any moment a recruit may be asked to repeat the D.I.'s last sentence, or else. Furthermore, the recruits are called upon to participate in the discussion and made to think about, and to personalize, the whole idea of sexual harassment. Private Jones, for example, might be asked to give an example in his own words. He might respond by creating a scenario in which a Marine repeatedly makes crude comments to his female counterpart—at which point the drill instructor might demand, "Jones, what kind of Marine would go around making another Marine uncomfortable?" ("A bad one, Sir!").

Similar sexual harassment training is simultaneously taking place on the women's side of the fence. The only difference is that the D.I. is a woman. This is another Marine Corps tradition. Recognizing at least the theoretical potential for complications in cross-sex training, the Corps has men teach men and women teach women. The woman drill instructor is equally as competent as the male D.I., fully as proud, and just as tough. No man in his wildest dreams would attempt to force his attentions upon a woman D.I.—not simply because he might find himself on report (or on his backside) but because of her dignity and bearing.

Her woman recruits must participate, as well, in interactive discussion groups. They are taught to recognize sexual harassment, rebuff it, and report it—and to refrain from such unwelcome behavior themselves. Of course, the daily regimen itself—such as shooting the M-16 rifle, crawling through the muddy, barbed-wire machine gun obstacle course, and learning self-defense—tends to produce a rather assertive, confident woman, who in no way resembles the "victim" profile.

Just as the men are taught to shave and dress properly, the woman recruits are shown how to apply cosmetics "the Marine Corps way." There is a manual for everything in the Corps, including the proper wearing of lipstick and nail polish. The formal, tersely written policy would no doubt amuse many young women in the outside world, as it dictates skirt lengths (slightly below the knee), nail lengths (no longer than a quarter inch from the tip of the finger), hair styles (on the short side), and earrings acceptable to the Corps (diminutive pearls are OK, only one per ear). But the message is quite serious—Marines, regardless of sex, are expected to put forth the right public image, and those who do not comply with Marine Corps standards are ordered to change their ways.

By the time the Marines graduate, they have become confident young men and women who enjoy a great deal of self-esteem and pride of membership. The women and the men Marines, in their sharp graduation uniforms, look upon each other as equals, each deserving of respect—and a shared sense of equality and mutual respect are certainly not the conditions that would encourage offensive behavior. Graduation day probably represents a high point in terms of the improbability of an incident taking place, but the sexual harassment training does not stop there. Marine Corps policy requires the discussion groups to continue throughout one's career, at the very least once a year.

Given all these precautions, are there incidents of sexual harassment reported in the Marine Corps? Unfortunately, yes, but the number of complaints filed is proportionately much smaller to those filed in the other branches of the service. Each report is fully investigated by an equal opportunity counselor—a career Marine dedicated to examining discrimination and harassment complaints. The responsible party is dealt with in a number of ways, ranging from psychological counseling, to dishonorable discharge, to jail time. The fact that these incidents occur, albeit far less frequently, in an organization that conscientiously tries to discourage such behavior is testimony to the difficulty of preventing sexual harassment. If it can happen in the Marine Corps, it can happen in any company.

Certainly the comparatively open, friendly workplace is much more conducive to the kind of behavior that would constitute sexual harassment than in the tightly regimented Corps. Young men and women who have had no formal training on the issue find themselves together in a fairly unrestricted, genial environment. Everybody dresses to look his or her best. (Of course, Marines want to look their best, too, but that usually means starched camouflage "utilities" and polished combat boots.) Many companies, while having a dress code on paper, are loathe to enforce it, especially when it comes to women's clothing. It is much easier for a male manager to tell a man he cannot wear jeans to work than to tell a woman that her skirt to is too high.

There is also in the workplace that curious mixture of courtesy and patronization that most women abhor. A man who is staggering under the weight of an armload of files will nonetheless struggle to open the door for an empty-handed woman with his foot. If she wears a flattering dress to work, she may have to endure the admiring inspection of her manager ("Helen, you really look good in that."). If she attempts to lift a few reams of paper, he comes to her "rescue." Instead of a pat on the back for a job well done, she receives instead an arm around the shoulders. Many women, fearing to appear rude—especially to a superior—put up with this kind of solicitude, which unfortunately may be interpreted as a "green light" for more of the same.

When the pattern of behavior becomes intolerable and the woman employee leaves the company, it is usually the company—not the offending party—that suffers the most. The transgressor may lose his job, but it is the corporation that is sued for not having taken the necessary steps to prevent sexual harassment in its workplace. Fear of litigation has forced many companies to pay huge insurance premiums to protect themselves from the damages that may follow a single complaint.

We believe the best insurance is a firm, proactive sexual harassment policy like the one implemented in the Marine Corps. Instead of simply requiring every employee to sign a form—out of so many other unread forms—acknowledging acceptance of the company's sexual harassment policy, management might follow the Marine Corps' model of interactive discussion groups. Possessing a signed piece of paper from every employee may help the company's legal position in case of a suit, but it does not constitute training. Management will never be confident that the message is really getting through unless it hears, in the words of its employees, their understanding of what is, and what is not, sexual harassment. Men and women alike must be guided into considering the unhappy predicament of the victim of unwanted attention; and the only way to awaken that kind of empathy is to have the employee vocalize how he or she would feel in such an uncomfortable situation.

Managers must not be shy about enforcing dress codes for either gender. Certainly this can be done with tact, but, lacking results, the manager must not compromise. The company is paying salaries to its personnel, and it is entitled to expect each individual to present a public image consistent with the corporate message. The company, like the Marine Corps, must also consider its women employees to be equals in every sense of the word, and, moreover, to be leaders. That means they must be treated accordingly. A Marine commander does not consider the gender of a Marine when a task must be assigned, in fact he may not even be aware that Private Smith is a woman. The business manager must be equally oblivious to gender. If all of his subordinates are equals, why would gender be of the slightest relevance?

Most important, the manager must lead by example on this issue. He, of course, must show no favoritism. When a woman enters his office, his door should remain open. Bawdy jokes and suggestive innuendoes around the water cooler must not be tolerated, either in single-sex groups or in mixed company. This does not mean the manager can walk away, good-naturedly shaking his head and proclaiming his neutrality; it means that he must, like the Marine officer, forcefully discourage humor of a sexual nature in his workplace. No employee should feel as if he could take his manager aside to whisper a ribald story he heard the night before. It is important to note that the Marine officer does not blame Marine Corps policy for his inability to join in the "fun"; he frowns upon anything that might jeopardize mission readiness—men and women Marines must be free of resentment and feelings of victimization. Similarly, the manager must create a culture in which such negative behavior is literally considered a form of sabotage.

Leadership Strategies Checklist

—Recognize that gender has absolutely nothing to do with leadership.
—Create a corporate culture of scrupulous equality.
—Realize that every leadership principle in this book applies to women associates, managers, and executives as well as men.

7

Leading to Victory: Ten Winning Strategies

"The most important responsibility we have to the American people is to win the nation's battles. We must be ready at a moment's notice to go anywhere, against any foe, to fight and WIN!"

—General Charles Krulak, Commandant, USMC

"Victory in the marketplace is only realized if it is sustainable. Personal leadership at every level is required to keep that momentum."

—Frederick Lopez, Department Manager Software Systems, Raytheon, currently Brigadier General, USMCR

The Commandant of the Marine Corps himself has said that the Corps exists for one purpose, and one purpose only: to win America's battles. He does not say to "fight" America's battles, but to "win." Marines are taught from Day One that victory is expected of them and that the Corps is of no use to America if it does not prevail on the battlefield. The Marine Corps really cannot afford to lose. Apart from the impact on the security of the nation, the Corps must also be concerned with its own destiny. As the smallest branch of the armed forces, it is the most vulnerable to a "hostile takeover" by the army or navy and must continue to justify its separate existence with a continuous record of victories. The Marine Corps has fulfilled its mission for two centuries, developing, along the way, strategies for victory that will be of interest to business leaders at all levels of responsibility.

Unlike the Marines, businesspeople are always "at war"—so much so that the critics of capitalism have traditionally characterized the competition of the marketplace as "dog-eat-dog," or "the big fish eating the little fish." While true enough in terms of the survivalist attitude that is required, this is an inaccurate description. In business, the big dogs or big fish do not always prevail; it is often the smartest that wins. CEOs, managers, and employees who can outthink the competition often do not have to outwork them. And the Marine Corps, which has often been at a numerical disadvantage on the battlefields, wrote the book on how to be one step ahead of the opponent.

Leadership has a purpose. We expect all the resources—human and material—invested in the building and mentoring of our leaders to culminate in a win. We do not want to be "led" into defeat. The ten Marine Corps principles that follow will help anyone who must inspire and direct his or her personnel toward unequivocal victory, whatever the circumstances, wherever the playing field.

Instill Courage

Of all the virtues, bravery is the one that, in reality, least resembles the ideal. We read about heroic deeds or watch them acted out in movies, and we can rather easily imagine ourselves being brave. But, suddenly finding ourselves in a position where courage must be summoned up, we would rather be anywhere else: we don't feel brave at all; we feel nauseated with fear. The expressions "weak-kneed," "shaking in my boots," "cold feet," and "scared sick" all aptly describe the physical conditions under which we must somehow have courage. The irony is appalling: we desperately need strength, but we are nearly crippled with fear; even panic would be an improvement, with its sudden burst of energy. At such times, we may look about for someone who is not afraid, someone who is "brave."

The Marine Corps knows that no such person exists. Everyone who must exhibit courage also feels the debilitating effects of fear. Even that competent warrior on the Marine recruiting poster will be frightened before battle, as will his buddies. But, like his buddies, he will remember his training and overcome his fear.

The ability to overcome fear is a prerequisite of effective leadership, in battle or in business. The Marine Corps teaches its own how to "be brave"; managers can do the same, using the same techniques.

The Marine Corps begins its training by presupposing the presence of fear in its recruits. But, rather than trying to calm down the young men and women who have just gotten off the bus, the drill instructors in every way heighten the anxiety of each recruit. They know full well these young people have, up to now, followed a rational policy of avoiding the discomfort of fear. But the D.I.s also know that, without the presence of fear, courage cannot be cultivated. The recruits who enter boot camp may be adventurous and hardy, but no life experiences have adequately prepared them for the horrors of infantry combat. They must experience fear beforehand and learn to function in its constant presence. The Marine Corps, therefore, systematically puts its people through a lot of frightening experiences.

Although the training may sometimes appear haphazard to the recruits—with much shouting and rushing about—the drill instructors carefully monitor each obstacle, knowing when to yell at a recruit and when to remain silent. The recruits learn to master their fear through a process that is (1) progressively more difficult, (2) designed for the group, and (3) mandatory.

Every leadership skill in boot camp is learned incrementally, including the control of fear. The tallest obstacles in the confidence course, for example, are preceded by smaller ones so that the recruit literally works his way up. Rappelling skills are learned in three stages, beginning with a scaffold only three feet off the ground, followed by a twenty-foot rope climb, and culminating in a heart-in-the-mouth walk down a sheer wall fifty feet high, without safety nets. Bayonet fighting is learned initially by practicing against a motionless dummy, then against a live partner (with pugil sticks), then against two and, finally, three adversaries. Aerobic training begins with a race around the barracks and ends, months later, with ten- and fifteen-mile cross-country runs, in full combat gear. With each level, the recruit's confidence grows. Having gone this far, he knows he can go a little farther.

All events are completed as a group, for a number of reasons, in addition to efficiency: (1) the recruit can see for himself that everyone else is doing what he fears, (2) he doesn't want to disgrace himself in front of his buddies, and (3) the team spirit creates a momentum of its own, sometimes sweeping the individual through the dreaded obstacle even before he realizes it.

Finally, all events are mandatory. The recruit, having no option but to participate, sets his mind to the task. One sees a lot of grim, determined faces on the fifty-foot stairway leading up to Hell Hole—an opening through which all will leap, one after the other, in a simulation of rappelling from a helicopter.

It is significant that, whatever the skill to be learned, the recruit is first "shown how" by the one man he simultaneously fears and admires the most: his drill instructor. The D.I., incidentally, could be a bystander; the classes are taught by full-time instructors and do not require his participation. But, by being the first man to accept each challenge, he solidifies his position as the role model throughout boot camp, excelling at every skill that, at the time, seems so impossibly complex to the recruit. Some D.I.s take this responsibility to the extreme. During the "dirtiest" event of the Crucible—the machine gun course, in which the recruit must crawl on his belly through fifty yards of wet, muddy trenches and barbed wire—it is not uncommon to see a drill instructor crawling through the mud himself, to buoy the morale of his platoon.

After boot camp, and for the remainder of their careers, Marines will participate in constant maneuvers. Although they are "only" drills, the realism is so intense that the peacetime Marines subconsciously become veterans. Fear of the unknown may be the greatest contributor to the anxiety felt on the eve of battle. Strenuous maneuvers with live ammunition and with participants who, by the look of them, believe it's the real thing, serve to demystify the unknown. In addition to the personal sense of confidence gained through maneuvers, Marines also see that the organization itself will never let them down. They know they will be materially supported in combat. The ammunition, food, and water, may run low, but in all likelihood, the big planes and helicopters will be there in time to resupply those on the ground.

Courage is also cultivated by the general state of combat readiness maintained on a Marine Corps base. The constant training, after all, has a purpose. Marines are constantly reminded that they will be the first to fight. Mobilization drills, officer briefings on trouble spots around the globe, antiterrorist exercises, all create a kind of Code Red mentality. Knowing that he may soon be in combat gives a Marine an attitude that is much less predisposed to fear.

Finally, the Marine Corps creates a martial culture in which courage is expected. Everybody is physically fit—it's hard to be brave when one is sobbing for oxygen after running out of the landing craft. Medals for bravery are worn on the chest, for all to see. Courageous Marines are memorialized; streets are named after heroes; plaques, statues, and portraits of famous Marines abound, reminding one of the fighting spirit that must be upheld. Everyone's office is decorated with combat photographs, flags, and battle mementos. "War stories" are passed on to the next generation, like the legends of old. After visiting a Marine Corps base for a few days, one begins to wonder if many of these modern warriors do not harbor a secret belief in a kind of Marine Valhalla, up in the sky.

One would think that the continual exposure to stress during a Marine's career would produce a stern, tense individual who grimly awaits the next challenge. But nothing could be further from the truth. Marines, as a group, are cheerful and robust. In fact their high spirits are in direct proportion to the challenges they have overcome. The more veteran the Marine, the more free from fear he is likely to be. The more free from fear he is, the happier the Marine.

Certainly courage—and sometimes a great deal of it—is required in the world of business. It takes courage to inform a customer of a price hike, or of a slippage in the delivery schedule, or of a product defect. It takes courage to take the company into uncharted waters or to refuse to give into an unjustified discrimination lawsuit. And sometimes it takes courage just to get up in the morning and go to work.

Managers who want to cultivate courage in themselves and in their personnel must first recognize that there is quite a bit of fear behind the smiling demeanor of the workplace. We worry about losing an important contract, or losing our jobs, even losing our homes. We must compete not only with outside competitors but sometimes with those in our own company who covet our title. We have anxiety about performing—not only at our daily duties, but also at special, high-profile assignments, such as major presentations or speeches.

Dare a manager actually add to this burden of worry? In a way, yes. After all, he and the drill instructor are after the same outcome: confident, happy personnel who have learned to master their fear. But, because very few of his subordinates will voluntarily place themselves in situations that cause performance anxiety, very few will ever consciously overcome their fear. Like the D.I., the manager must put himself and his people through progressively challenging courage-building experiences. He must make these a mandatory group experience, and he must lead the way.

Of course, there won't be a fifty-foot wall to rappel, but every one of his subordinates will have obstacles that seem, to them, just as daunting. Rather than trying to customize the "bravery exercises" to each individual, he has only to single out a fear that is shared by all. Often the conquest of a big phobia overcomes other, smaller fears by default.

The fear of public speaking is certainly the most likely candidate for a major, almost universal fear. Psychologists maintain that, next to the fear of death, it is the most widely held phobia in the industrialized world. People who have confronted this fear, and have learned to master it, find that their new confidence manifests itself in every other facet of the professional and personal lives. Managers who hold weekly meetings in which everyone takes on progressively more difficult speaking or presentation assignments will see personalities revolutionized before their eyes. Speakers who trudge toward the podium as if it were a scaffold walk away proud of themselves and liberated from performance anxiety.

Managers can create a "culture of courage" within their departments in much the same way as the fighting spirit is maintained in the Marine Corps. Acts of courage—such as taking an ethical stand against the use of insider information, resisting the inappropriate overtures of an important supplier, or stepping outside the chain of command to address a potential product flaw—should be rewarded. Innovative and proactive approaches to customers who are tied to the competition should be lauded and written up in the company newsletter.

While applauding actual acts of bravery, the manager can create situations, through realistic role play and simulation exercises, in which associates act out coping strategies for use with difficult customers or deal with internal crises such as production failures and delivery lapses. If he runs a sales department, an impromptu day of cold calls with one of the reps will make his established accounts seem like pussycats. If he heads a service department, he and his technician must visit the Customer From Hell and listen to the tirade. The manager should constantly be telling war stories to his associates about how current and past employees have pushed themselves outside the comfort zone and found, literally, a "brave new world."

It is interesting to note that, in the Marine Corps, courage is always a virtue, even when it is not associated with victory. Indeed, some of the bravest acts are—in terms of the immediate battle—seemingly futile. Legendary last stands, such as the Marine defense of Wake Island during World War II, for example, ended in the defeat of those we memorialize today.

Unfortunately, management does not always recognize courage as a virtue. While it is eager to praise the determination that gained a customer, management occasionally punishes the courageous individual who has lost a customer. The salesman, for example, who steadfastly holds to the price of his product and tries to sell the company's commitment to quality and service is going to lose a customer now and then. A service technician who politely refuses to honor the warranty of a piece of equipment that has been grossly "modified" by the customer will probably elicit complaints. A production supervisor who refuses to promise the impossible and insists upon an aggressive but realistic product delivery schedule will occasionally lose an order. But all who have shown "backbone" will serve the company well in the long term. That kind of courage must never be punished if management hopes to create spirited, confident employees.

Of course, management's backbone must be equally stiff. The individual employee who was justified in tactfully resisting the demands of a bullying customer must be supported by the company. Nothing will make a coward out of somebody more quickly than having the rug pulled out from under him by the very people he represents. Conversely, if his instructions from the manager were to agree with the customer's demands, the company must be prepared to back him up with the necessary resources to fulfill his promise; without it, he becomes a fall guy for a manager who wanted to bring in the order, knowing full well that the customer would be strung along by a production and delivery schedule that was less than adequate. Just as the Marine gains courage from ships, jets, and helicopters committed to supporting him, the employee must have a similar faith that his company will be there to support him.

Study the Past

At Officer Candidate School, the young recruits may study—in the same day—space-age technology, such as the Global Positioning System, and the tactical innovations of a military commander from antiquity, like Hannibal, who repeatedly defeated the Roman army two thousand years ago. Each class is taught with equal fervor; and, as far as the instructors are concerned, both are equally relevant.

To the Marine officer, classic battles of the past are not simply "brandy-and-cigar" after-dinner topics; they are vital, hip pocket reference points for the present. The officer's bayonet may be the only weapon he has in common with the infantryman of the past, but the ancient principles of maneuver can be just as relevant on the vastly changed battlefield of today. He is quite aware that the mistakes of the past can be reenacted, even by a state-of-the-art military force; and he doesn't want it to be his.

The Marine officer is not dazzled by technology. He is an expert in modern warfare, of course, but his knowledge is also grounded in fundamentals of military science that have not changed for ages. While all of the branches of the armed forces share the same state-of-the-art technology, Marine Corps training goes on in much the same way as it has for generations. Despite its capacity for rapid mechanized deployment, the Corps expects its Marines to be able to move the old-fashioned way—by running, in full combat gear, over any kind of terrain. Even with all of the modern battlefield communication technologies, Marines are frequently tested for their knowledge of arm and hand signals. And, although each Marine is armed with the most sophisticated personal weaponry, he is also trained in the lost arts of knife fighting and hand to hand combat. He is even trained to use his rifle as a club.

This emphasis on retaining the fighting skills of the past is unique to the Marine Corps, and the training may appear a bit anachronistic to the visitor. Marine generals know that, with today's technology, the odds of their Marines finding themselves in a situation in which they must engage the enemy on the most primitive level are very slim. But they also know that computers do occasionally crash, satellite transmissions can be garbled, and troops can be temporarily cut off from support and run out of ammunition. If the mission is to be successful, Marines must be able to fall back on training that prepared them even for this unlikely scenario. Take away his satellites, his battlefield computers, and his "smart" weapons systems, and the Marine will still beat you.

The Marine officer's enthusiasm for the past also applies to the origin and genealogy of his own unit. He makes certain that the men in his tactical organization—whether infantry, tanks, helicopters, or jets—are well aware of its colorful history. Familiarity with the heritage of the unit can have a profound effect on the Marines who now have the honor to serve in it. There is a great sense of pride, certainly, but also the sobering obligation to continue the winning tradition of one's predecessors. That sense of obligation applies not only to the battlefield; many a young Marine has refrained from after-hours excesses, not wanting to sully the record of his unit—in uniform, or out of uniform.

Capitalism has been around only a comparatively short time, yet—if the articles in the business sections of magazines and newspapers are any indication—its past is more deeply buried than the ancient civilizations that seem to fascinate so many of us. Many businessmen and women—especially those who are the most comfortable with the spectacular technology available today—seem to regard the modern era as completely unprecedented.

Today's executive sits at a virtual command center. His desktop PC is linked, through a wide area network, to hundreds of "peer" computers within the company—each as powerful as the huge mainframes of yesterday. His business communications are sent via on-line electronic e-mail across the vast Internet with the speed of telepathy. With the push of a button, he can host video conference calls and see, as well as hear, participants from all over the globe. What could he possibly learn from even the tycoons of the nineteenth century, who, by today's standards, ruled very primitive business kingdoms?

The manager who, like Scrooge, tries to ignore the "Ghost of Business Past" may find himself haunted by mistakes he could have avoided had he studied the rich legacy of his predecessors. The great capitalists of America's industrial past— Jay Gould, John Jacob Astor, Herbert Dow, Henry Ford, John D. Rockefeller, John Pierpont Morgan, Andrew Carnegie, Bernard Baruch, and others—almost exclusively came from poor, even destitute, backgrounds. They put in hours at the office that would make the modern workaholic throw in the towel. They risked their fortunes, and at times their lives, on truly unprecedented ventures. Without historical guidance, they made mistakes, recovered, and eventually triumphed. Besides making themselves wealthy, they enriched the quality of life for all Americans. Yet, many executives today would be hard pressed to recount any significant details of the struggles of these pioneers—details that may be quite relevant in their own business lives.

A poster in most Marine recruiting offices shows a drawing of Marines "hitting the beach." The Marine in front is wearing modern combat dress and holding an M-16 rifle; the Marines behind him are wearing various battle uniforms and gear from the American Revolution, the War of 1812, Spanish-American War, and other wars, all the way up to the present. The message is dramatically clear: the modern Marine didn't just appear out of the blue; he is a perpetuation of the Marines who defended America long before him—no better and no worse.

Similarly, the modern workplace is not unprecedented, nor are the managers and personnel who work within it. The fundamentals of business have not changed over the years.

Successful companies exist today, as they did yesterday, for one purpose: to serve the customer. A contract is still an exchange of trust, despite all the modern boilerplate to protect each party. Honesty, integrity—and a keen eye for their opposites in the marketplace—remain the most important qualities in inter-personal dealings. Mistakes and miscalculations are based on the same, very human impulses that motivated the ill-advised executive decisions of the past. The government is still capable of regulating business growth, as it did with the railroad and steel companies generations ago. And hard work is still the best policy in any industry.

The skills of "business past" should not be underestimated, either. Our fascination with, and reliance upon, the technology at our fingertips can actually hinder customer relations. The executive who is in the habit of communicating via e-mail may have forgotten the emotional impact of a handwritten letter—not to mention a personal visit. The salesman who relies exclusively upon professional, multimedia presentations—replete with video, music, colorful graphs, and pie charts—is allowing a "light show" to do his talking for him. He may never have bothered to develop the public speaking skills needed to communicate directly with his audience and to differentiate himself from all the other salesmen in the business world who hide behind similar, high-tech presentations. It doesn't occur to him that, by turning down the lights in the conference room and directing the audience's attention to a screen on the wall, he has abrogated his responsibility as the company rep. By turning the room into a kind of home theater, he has lost control of his audience. Without intuitive feedback from the faces in the dark, he has no idea what the individuals who sit there passively watching the screen are thinking. He cannot see which product features and benefits are hitting home and which ones are raising questions and concerns. It doesn't occur to him that these people might be delighted if he simply took over the presentation and spoke to them as human beings. It is ironic that the biggest fear of such a salesman is that his software might crash, leaving him exposed on stage without the technology he depends upon—when that is the very condition most conducive to true communication.

In our age of technology worship, esoteric acronyms and buzzwords confuse and intimidate many customers, who long for unpretentious, honest speech. Reference points are lost; a new associate out of college may not know what the boss means by cautioning him not to produce an "Edsel," asking him to "railroad" something through, or asking him to bring his "slide-rule." Writing, too, is becoming a lost art. The business letters of the past were works of art compared to the communiqués of today. Many executives, who have lost the skill of expressing their thoughts on paper rely on the computer's "grammar check"—and end up not understanding what they themselves have written. The document is submitted, anyway, because, if the computer says it's correct, it must be correct.

The business skills that served our predecessors so well have not been rendered obsolete by the tools we have available to us today; they have been enhanced. The Marine does not discount his high-tech advantage over the enemy; nor should the manager. But the manager must remember that the customer is not the enemy. His dealings with the customer should be as low-tech as possible—that is, he should relate on a warm, personal, human level and use the space-age weaponry on his competitors.

Create a Sense of Mission

Public opinion on the military fluctuates in proportion to the popular support for its conflicts. During a long career, a professional soldier may find that his troops are actually scorned by some of their own countrymen—as in the case of the returning veterans of Vietnam—and later hailed as conquering heroes, like the triumphant Americans who paraded back from Desert Storm. Abroad, in third-world countries where our servicemen and women live on bases or visit from aircraft carriers, the reception from the "locals" can be varied, as well.

Not everyone understands or appreciates the sacrifices made by the members of today's services; and the sacrifices of yesteryear are remembered mainly because the military itself ceremonializes significant past events. If it were left to the general public to keep the memories of Bunker Hill, Gettysburg, the Alamo, Flanders Field, Pearl Harbor, and D day alive, it is a matter of conjecture just how long these traditions would be continued. Every new generation is, understandably, caught up in its own time; the stories of their parents are often considered self-serving moralistic exaggerations. The incomparable exploits of the World War II generation, for example, are sometimes lumped into the same category as "walking a mile to school every day in the snow." Not having experienced the acute danger of those years, the sons and daughters smile indulgently at the reminiscences of their parents, or grandparents.

Even the legendary Marine Corps has seen its stock rise and fall in the hearts and minds of the people it is working so hard to protect. Anything that threatens the morale of its Marines, on or off the base, is always a matter of concern to the leadership within the Corps. Most Marines are young and, though they would be the last to admit it, sensitive to the response from the public. A young man who has recently met all the challenges of boot camp and now proudly walks the streets of his home town in his brand-new uniform is at risk of being deflated by the indifferent or disparaging glance of an attractive young woman. He may encounter citizens who do not at all appreciate or understand what he has gone through. It may even seem to him as if the very people he is "doing it all for" do not care, never having asked him to "do it" in the first place. He may return to his base dispirited, determined to take his next weekend leave dressed in civilian clothes. And, later, when the time comes to reenlist, he may even feel he has wasted the past four years.

The challenge faced by the Marine Corps is to somehow keep up the drum beat of boot camp so that every Marine, at any stage in his or her career, feels as if he or she is doing the most important job in the world, whether or not those "on the outside" always appreciate it. That is why Marines are constantly reminded by their own leadership of the vital significance of their mission and of the importance of each individual's role within that mission. And although the Marine Corps has a relatively large "workforce" (compared to many companies) of 175,000 members, the individual Marine does not feel lost. In fact, every infantryman is told time and again that he is the focus of the entire organization, that all the ships and jets and personnel in the great assembly of power that precedes an amphibious landing, exist for one reason and one reason only—to support him on the battlefield. He is conscious of being the very symbol of victory; the battle is not won until the Marine on the ground says it is.

A young private who earns what amounts to minimum wage nevertheless feels that he is a significant contributor to a great cause. He feels important as a human being, as an infantryman, and as a member of an organization with a glorious history. Not a day goes by when he is not in some manner exalted by the Marine Corps. The very mission statement of officer training is "to prepare newly commissioned officers to lead our most precious asset: the enlisted Marine." Thousands of Marines reenlist every year knowing full well that an easier way of life, and certainly a more lucrative career, could be theirs for the asking on the outside. But many feel that their jobs are simply too important to leave in somebody else's hands.

Simultaneously, the Marine Corps is also doing its best to make sure that the surrounding community appreciates its Marines. "Open house" days on the base, air shows, parades, Toys for Tots Christmas drives, recruiters on high school and college campuses, and volunteer disaster relief efforts both educate and serve the community and help to pave the way for the individual Marine's excursions into it. But, if for some reason, society at large does not always quite appreciate his sacrifices at home or abroad, the Marine will find that "back home" on the base, he is considered a VIP.

If a company could create that kind of self-esteem within the workplace, it could be confident that its employees, while "on the outside," would not be as vulnerable to such demoralizing influences as peer disdain of their jobs, suggestions from the spouse that he or she could do better somewhere else, or outright competitive offers. Surveys reveal that many Americans tend to exaggerate their importance when talking to people outside their employment. A receptionist, for example, may describe her duties to friends as those of an executive secretary; a factory assembler who takes the bus to work may carry his lunch in a briefcase rather than a brown bag and then leave the briefcase in his locker all day; a salesman may shudder at the term "sales" and refer to himself instead as an "account executive." Many of us exaggerate in order to feel better about ourselves. In our society, in which status is so often linked to income—or the symbols of high incomes, such as the luxury automobiles many drive but cannot afford—there are many people who are not particularly proud of what they do for a living. And if a paycheck is the only bond holding an employee to the organization, that company can expect a lot of costly turnover.

At work, an employee may feel as if he is simply a number, lost and anonymous in a vast corporate structure. He may feel that anybody could do his job and is, in fact, reminded of precisely that by his manager, who dangles the paycheck in front of him to spur performance. When "the suits" come to visit his department, they may not remember his first name, or his duties, or his history with the company. On the shifts when he must work overtime to finish an emergency order, he may find that the manager has not stayed after hours with the "troops." His efforts may be unappreciated not only at work but at home, as well. His wife may resent the "exploitation" by the company and suggest that his bachelor co-workers could have just as easily stayed late without him. When he tries to explain the urgency of the situation, he is at a sudden loss for words, not really believing in it himself.

The company faces a challenge similar to the one facing

the Marine Corps, which is to instill a sense of mission in its employees that will carry them through not only the workday but after hours, as well. Every associate must be proud of what he or she does and feel an integral part of the "big picture" that has been clearly painted by management. The employee must be reminded daily, in one form or another, that he is important to the company and to the customers who are depending upon him. He must be reminded that his success at work is important to his family and even to the community at large. Management should let its workforce know, for example, that the company pours thirty million dollars worth of payroll into the local economy every year, as well as twelve million tax dollars that help build and maintain the roads, bridges, and schools of the community. The employee should be reminded that, out of all the applicants for his job, "We picked you." He should feel that the company would be wounded if he left and hard pressed to find an adequate replacement. Instead of being told by his manager that he is "dispensable," he should be told, like the Marine, that he is indispensable.

Keep Goals Realistic

Sometimes a very high degree of esprit de corps, while appreciated by commanders, must be governed with realistic assignments. A platoon of approximately fifty Marines just might be crazy enough to take on a company of two hundred enemy soldiers, but chances are their Marine officers will await reinforcements or change the assignment from attacking to "harassing" the enemy. The adage "Be careful what you tell a Marine to do, because he will die trying" is always in the back of the mind of every commanding officer, who may sometimes find himself in the ironic position of trying to protect his Marines from their own unbounded confidence. Experienced leaders know that even a poorly trained enemy—in sufficient numbers and under unforeseen (and unforeseeable) circumstances—can defeat even the best troops. A tragic example of this occurred during the October 1993 relief effort in Somalia. Eighteen of the army's elite Rangers were killed, and seventy-three soldiers, including members of the ultra-secret Delta Force anti-terrorist command, were wounded in the Battle of Mogadishu by a large mob of untrained hoodlums with automatic weapons. And no one thought of the Panamanian Self Defense Forces as a particularly effective military organization either, yet the lives of four navy Seals—extraordinarily tough "special-operations" commandos—were lost during the first hour of the American attack on Panama at the end of the regime of General Manuel Noriega.

So Marine commanders, while determined to bring every mission to a successful conclusion, try to keep the mission itself achievable. No enemy is underestimated, and the capability of the Marines is not overestimated. If, for example, the assignment is unusually daunting, Marine generals are not shy about asking for the necessary additional resources that will give their troops on the battlefield the greatest chances for success. Marines are not sent into combat without the proper tools for the job.

Marines believe in their leadership and in the feasibility of the plans their officers will come up with to complete the mission—in part because these same officers will go into battle with them. Every experienced Marine knows that, in combat, nothing is guaranteed. He is confident, however, that his assigned goals are attainable—and that they have been assigned by the very officers who will lead the way. He knows, furthermore, that these officers will never intentionally put him in a position to fail.

If the consequences of overly ambitious, unrealistic expectations from upper management were to cost the very lives of its employees, as can happen in actual combat, perhaps the corporate goals of many companies would be less capricious. As it is, CEOs have no problem presenting to their boards of directors "bullish," and aggressive growth plans that sometimes more than double the growth rates of the previous year.

Many in upper management seem to believe that aiming high is a harmless policy and that, if employees are forced to "reach for the stars," they will, at the very least, touch the moon.

But unrealistic and unreachable goals can have destructive consequences. By raising the bar to impossible heights, in the hope that performance will be proportionately improved over the year before, management is setting its workplace up for a fall. Never having met its previous goals—and never having enjoyed the fruits of victory, such as a year-end bonus—the workforce will consider each new set of expectations from management to be predictably unreachable, and even hilarious. Year after year of failing to achieve the corporation's goals will bias its employees toward failure. Cynicism will set in, not only among the employees, who suspect the company of purposely denying the possibility of performance bonuses, but also among upper management, which continues to set its expectations knowing full well they will not, and cannot, be met. Since management itself does not take its goals seriously enough to enforce them, no one is really held accountable, no heads roll, and the employees can see that they weren't honestly expected to meet the mark.

Employees, like Marines, must taste victory often if winning is to become habitual; for failure can become a habit, too—indeed, a way of life. Management will lose its rising stars, who will see that their income has been, for all intents and purposes, capped. The loss of top performers does not go unnoticed, incidentally, by the board of directors or by institutional stockholders, who have an intimate knowledge of the internal operations of the company.

An increase in expectations should always travel in both directions. Employees who are asked to do more look to management to provide them with the tools to achieve more. A sales force, for example, tasked with penetrating a new market, is entitled to the necessary support, in terms of: new product brochures, a marketing blitz that paves the way, advertising, telemarketing leads and surveys, and an infrastructure that has been ramped up to fulfill the new incoming orders. Many companies have no problem asking their employees to go the extra mile without budgeting for the commitment itself.

We are not suggesting that management take it easy on itself or on the workforce. Companies must grow, or they will perish. Reasonable annual increases by management are expected and will be accepted by a workforce still savoring the victory of the year before. But goals out of all proportion to the performance of the previous year will take the wind out of the corporate sails. So often a company asks for a 25 percent increase, when, if the truth were to be known, it expects 12 percent. And if, by year's end, gross sales are up by 15 percent, management, secretly delighted, will nonetheless be publicly "disappointed that our goals were not met." Ironically, the net annual growth could have been even higher than 15 percent had the goals been set lower, making prosperity for the company and its employees mutually achievable, as in a partnership. Employees who have a realistic potential of increasing their income by increasing their performance will unconsciously raise the bar themselves, by their own production. Otherwise, they find themselves damned if they do and damned if they don't—penalized for not achieving their targets by forfeiting the possibility of bonus, or penalized for achieving their goals by having them doubled the subsequent year.

Instill a Fighting-Man Culture

It must be remembered that, despite all the incidental benefits of being a Marine, such as character building and job training, the Marine Corps exists only to fight and win America's battles. Behind his good cheer and smiling face, the individual Marine is first and foremost a warrior. For his entire life in the Corps, he studies war, practices war, and—if there is a war—ardently wishes to be the first to fight. It is difficult to imagine a culture throughout history, including that of Prussia and that of the samurai, more devoted to the preparation for war.

Yet, in the Marine Corps, as in any organization, there is always the possibility that "whom you know may be more important than what you know." Many a career colonel has looked back upon his thirty years of service and wondered what he could have done differently to become a general. Of course, every career is unique, but surely there are some choices of duty that are more expedient, in terms of promotion, than others. Being assigned to the staff of an influential general, for example, may be a better career move than commanding a company of infantrymen in Bosnia or taking an assignment that is somewhat off the beaten path, such as serving in a secret special-warfare unit dedicated to combating terrorism. Many officers, young and full of vigor, nonetheless jump at the exciting combat commands, even though staff jobs might have been more personally advantageous in the long term.

These ambitious, tough officers tend to associate with others like them and tend to share similar career paths, which often dead-end at the very respectable rank of colonel, rather than general. They, along with the NCOs who have chosen the same rocky road, form the "fighting-man" culture within the Corps, while those who have chosen equally exciting tours of duty closer to the movers and shakers are known good-naturedly as "staff weenies." This is not to say that those who serve on staffs are not fighting men; every Marine is a rifleman first. But it could be said that they are a little less rough around the edges—with social graces developed by years of interacting with politicians, the media, and foreign dignitaries—than their counterparts who seem to revel in the discomforts of life in the field. These diplomatic skills are not to be underestimated, either. Besides fighting actual battles, those who become generals must also constantly fight on Capitol Hill to save the Marine Corps from being further downsized, or absorbed into the navy (or even, God forbid, the army!).

Businesses, too, have their "front lines"; but where the front lines actually are is dependent upon whom you talk to. Ask sales managers, and they will tell you that the entire support and production side of the company exists only because of sales. ("Nothing happens until somebody sells something.") Service managers claim that customer satisfaction is what makes the world go round, since unhappy customers will never buy again. Those on the production line ask rhetorically, "What would either department service or sell if there were no product?" And the IS (Information Systems) manager, who must maintain the security and the speed of the local-area network (LAN) within the facility, the wide-area network connecting branches coast to coast, the company Intranet for e-mail, and the Internet site on the World Wide Web, gazes down upon all departments from his position on a three-dimensional "front line" that didn't even exist a decade ago.

Though sales, service, production, and IS staff may argue about where the front line is, they would probably agree on where it is not. The hapless paper shufflers of order entry, the bean counters in accounting, the company's attorneys, engineers, ISO 9000 auditors, expense clerks, executive secretaries, and receptionists are not perceived to be on the front lines of the business battlefield. Their peers in the more stressful, vigorous departments think the "staff weenies" have a pretty cushy slot in the company, while they must spend each day in comparative "hand-to-hand combat," meeting quotas and deadlines, facing customers, and solving emergencies.

The managers who supervise those on the front line should continue to promote the fighting-man culture; it spurs performance, encourages competition, and creates the kind of esprit de corps that inspires individuals to go beyond themselves. Those who manage the "staff weenies" must be equally assertive. Every member of the organization is on the front line, and every position has its own unique challenges and pressures; the only people who have "got it soft" are the employees of the competition, who aren't fortunate enough to be working for the most aggressive, the most efficient, and the most demanding company in the industry.

There Is No "Peacetime"

History textbooks will no doubt regard the 1980s and 1990s as decades of relative calm, at least for Americans. There is no longer compulsory military service, and it would probably be the end of any politician's career to suggest that draft boards be reinstated. All branches of the military have been radically downsized. Even so, the occasional hot spots and skirmishes around the world confirm the unchallenged military superiority of Uncle Sam. With the collapse of the Soviet Union, the terrible specter of a third world war has vanished. Yet, upon visiting any Marine Corps base, one has the distinct impression that somebody forgot to tell it to the Marines.

A Marine Corps base is a kind of time warp back to the days when America was fighting for its very survival. Not only are realistic maneuvers going on all over the place, but the mind-set of the individuals one meets seems to be earnestly engaged in conflict. There is a sense of urgency that makes the visitor wonder if he missed some terrible announcement on the morning news.

Of course, there is a very practical reason for all the preparation going on: the Marines are literally the first to fight. In these two decades of comparative peace, Marines were dispatched to Bosnia, Somalia, Haiti, Iraq, Panama, and Grenada. And, if American citizens must be evacuated from a far-off country undergoing a revolution, it will be Marine helicopters that calm the evacuees' fears. War, or the preparation for war, is the Marine Corps way of life; there is, as far as Marines are concerned, no peacetime.

It is surprising that a business leader, who works in an even more hostile environment—where "peace" is never declared—allows himself to lose the competitive attitude for even one second. After all, there are people out there who are dedicated to taking away his customers, his market share, and his employees. Rather than one implacable foe, there are dozens, coming at him from all angles of attack (e.g., lower pricing, better service contracts, superior product features, more responsive on-line help, better delivery). He must worry about industrial espionage, the security on his wide-area network, and the research and development of the competition. Not only is he fighting for his business life; his customers are as well, and they may go out of business or be forced to find a more cost-effective vendor.

One would think that in this extremely competitive world, every company would be on a "war footing" every minute of the day. But the business sections of the newspapers are full of accounts of companies blindsided by the competition, unpleasantly surprised by the loss of key customer renewal orders or the resignation of top people, who have jumped ship to a competitor. Generally, it is not the young, struggling company but the more successful one that is most likely to take its customers, its market share, and its own employees for granted.

The Marine Corps is one of the most successful organizations of the past two hundred years; yet, to look at Marines during maneuvers, one would think they are fighting to keep their jobs. That kind of earnest effort is missing in more than one prominent business today. Upper management can keep its personnel in a state of readiness by making it clear to every associate just how inimical the world outside is to his company's, and to his own, well-being.

Just as in a military briefing, the strengths and weakness of the competition should be frankly discussed. During those companywide presentations where the CEO delights in pointing out the ascending growth indicators on the graph, the competition's growth should be reviewed as well, so that all associates can see the progress that has been made, in a sense, at their own expense. Just as Allied newsreels during World War II included information on enemy victories, internal corporate news letters should, as they trumpet company triumphs, also discuss what contracts were lost to the competition, and why. And every employee should be rid of the notion that "the market is big enough" for both him and his competition. When a Marine general addresses his men before battle, he does not wish both sides the best. He is out to vanquish the enemy. We are not suggesting that employees be rude or that salespeople "bad-mouth" the competition. We are suggesting, however, that every associate in the company dedicate himself to defeating his competitors with superior performance, not to coexisting with them eternally. "Market share" is a regrettable term; it implies that the market should, by its nature, be equitably divided. If Marine Corps generals looked at battles in terms of sharing successes with the enemy, the American public would be demanding new leadership.

Employees, incidentally, who are on a "war footing"— that is, filled with the competitive spirit—do not "burn out," or come to hate their jobs. On the contrary, competitive juices are the elixir of business life. A sense of urgency makes the day fly by; it's the deadly routine of the comfort zone that slows down the work day to eight agonizing hours. This does not mean that the workforce should never relax. A CEO wants his employees to stop and smell the flowers—especially the ones growing through the cracks at the abandoned sites of his former competitors.

Know Your Enemy

Even in the midst of a victory celebration, such as V-E Day, V-J Day, or, more recently, the jubilation following the stunning victory of the American-led forces in Desert Storm, the Joint Chiefs of Staff cast a wary eye on the horizon, wondering where the next threat will come from. It seems that the Pentagon has, over the years, developed a plan for fighting just about everybody; in fact, as recently as the beginning of World War I, there were contingency plans for war against, of all nations, Great Britain. Even today, we occasionally read about American citizens who have been accused of espionage by our allies; or, conversely, of agents of friendly countries caught spying on the United States military and on American corporations. It seems that all agencies charged with the defense of their respective nations begin with the premise that anybody could one day become an enemy.

The Marine Corps is very concerned about the "competition." The social, economic, political, and military characteristics of rogue nations and potential enemies are studied with diligence. Intelligence reports from agents who have spent years in the enemy's midst are analyzed. Well before it has been committed to action, the Marine Corps has developed a detailed dossier on the opposition. The enemy's military leaders are profiled. Marine intelligence officers become familiar with their opponents—where they studied the science of war, what strategic doctrines they were taught, and by which mentors. Once on the battlefield itself, satellite and fly-by information is plotted on the situation map. For a "worm's eye" view, Marine reconnaissance units infiltrate the front lines and compare perspectives. The early prisoners of war or eager "turncoats" are interrogated. Enemy radio and other electronic transmissions are intercepted and analyzed. The entire collage of information is pieced together at field headquarters, where a Marine general, still not satisfied, may commandeer a helicopter and be flown over the battle area himself. Before the shooting begins, he will know more about his enemy than he may about his best friend.

The other side of "knowing your enemy" is making sure he does not get to know you. Marine commanders try to constantly change the face of warfare so that the enemy—perhaps expecting a patented Marine Corps frontal assault—is surprised, instead, by a massive helicopter-borne infantry offensive behind its lines. Indeed, the doctrine of Marine "maneuver warfare" is so flexible that any opponent would be hard pressed to anticipate the Marine's next move. "Keeping them guessing" is a classic Marine Corps strategy. The very presence of Marines in the Desert Storm theater had the military advisers of Saddam Hussein absolutely convinced that an amphibious landing was imminent. This preoccupation diverted the energies of a large portion of his troops as they prepared for an attack from the sea that never came.

Businesses are, of course, very interested in their competition—some, unfortunately, to the point of reckless behavior. In January 1997, Volkswagen-AG and General Motors settled a lawsuit in which GM had sued for damages because of alleged industrial espionage. Within a year of GM's filing its lawsuit, Volkswagen had agreed to pay one hundred million dollars in damages and to purchase one billion dollars' worth of GM parts over the next seven years. (CNN Financial Network, 1/9/97) Many companies and individuals have found themselves on the wrong side of the jury box for attempting to illegally solicit sensitive information about their competition. Although a Marine, when captured, will give only his name, rank, and service number, an employee, when wined and dined by "the enemy," may sing like a canary. The information gained, however, is hardly worth the risk. There are many other ways—both legal and ethical—to find out about one's rivals.

Many companies conduct "opposition research" using every legitimate tool at their disposal. The Internet offers a wealth of information—and misinformation—consolidating a vast array of source material into a massive on-line database. Press releases, annual reports, stock analyses, 10-K and 10-Q reports from the Securities and Exchange Commission, the Web sites of your competitors, business "chat rooms," Dunn & Bradstreet and Moody company profiles—not to mention articles from trade publications, business journals, and newspapers—are literally at the fingertip of the patient and discriminating researcher. The doors of the library, the Patent Office, the local courthouse, and the International Trade Commission are open to all in search of business information. Conventions can be tremendous sources of information; one's competitors may play their cards close to the vest, but their new products and prototypes are on display, and discussions with the potential customers passing by are in earnest.

Another worthwhile pursuit can be reading the employment advertisements of business opponents; many ads are very specific in the descriptions of the skill sets required, giving an indication of the kinds of products they are ramping up for. Conversations with suppliers can be very profitable. If a supplier isn't also supplying one's competitor, he certainly hopes to and may have information he can ethically share.

But perhaps the most voluble source of information about the competition is his customers. Companies that are working with the opposition are all too often written off as hopeless prospects. But the purchasing agents of these companies have a fiduciary duty to their own organizations to consider your company as backup, should the situation suddenly turn. He will make an appointment with you, if only to confirm in his own mind that he is still getting the best deal from your rival. Many customers do not have to be coaxed into revealing information; they will positively brag about the ability of your competitor to meet their current and future needs. A great deal can be learned about planned upgrades, product releases, and exceptionally favorable terms and conditions. In addition, opportunities may suddenly appear; rarely is everything in a state of perfection. All may not be right in terms of service, or project management, or billing, or your competitor's ability to deliver the product on schedule. The customer may be guided into the realization that, as fond as he is of your rival, it is in his self-interest to have another resource at his beck and call. While establishing yourself as an alternative, eager to prove your worth in some small way, such as fulfilling even a token order, you may also walk away with timely information, ethically gained.

Of course, no one source of information is definitive in itself. The business leader, like the Marine officer, must piece together the disparate data to form a complete picture of his opponent's activities in the marketplace. While learning about him, he must simultaneously assume opposition research is being conducted about his own company, as well, and behave accordingly.

Rather than placing an employment ad for a very particular skill—which might tip one's hand to the competition—the resourceful executive may advertise for an individual who is knowledgeable in a category of disciplines, including the one actually desired. Or, if a company is developing three new products, management may decide to send out press releases on only two of them, throwing the competition on a scent that, while not false, hardly leads to the nest. And, whenever confronted by reporters who ask for a confirmation or denial of a rumor about one's company, perhaps the best policy is to always answer "No comment," whether the rumor is true or false; allowing the competition to speculate.

Are there "weapons" a business leader should not use? Our military, for example, has access to nuclear, biological, and chemical weapons that will probably (one hopes) never be employed. Similarly, an executive may, by pure serendipity, discover inside information from Wall Street or encounter a "turncoat" from his competition who is prepared to exchange sensitive information for a favor. All such temptations must, of course, be resisted. The ethical repercussions can cause great damage to his company's reputation—with its peers in the industry, its stockholders, its customers, and its lenders. Legal repercussions can literally bankrupt the organization. The business leader, like the Marine officer, must always abide by the rules of "war."

Command From a Forward Position

It is said that Alexander the Great's soldiers begged him not to ride into battle in the lead chariot, as was his custom. Marine Corps officers would blush at the comparison, but historically they have always led the old-fashioned way—in front. In every war, Marine officers have suffered a higher casualty rate than their counterparts in the army infantry. The Marine Corps' philosophy has always been to command from a forward position, which means from the thick of it.

Of course, this is a great motivator for the troops, who see their officers, who certainly could have remained in the rear directing the attack, instead accompany them, shoulder to shoulder, into harm's way. But there is another reason, as well, for the aggressiveness of the Marine Corps officer. He wants real-time information. He wants to see for himself, through the fog of war, what the enemy is up to. There is simply no better way to command troops in combat. Of course, the high command can see developments (e.g., from satellite reconnaissance) that the officer in the trenches cannot. But no soldier will ever be inspired to advance into a hail of bullets by orders phoned in on the radio from the safety of a remote command post; he is inspired to follow the officer in front of him.

Business managers must recognize the identical principle: it is much more effective to get your personnel to follow you than to push them forward from behind a desk. Whatever the area of responsibility—sales, production, service—the manager must lead from a forward position. The more important the mission, the more important it is to be at the front. All too often, the walls of his office isolate the manager from the battlefield of the marketplace, from his customers, and from his own personnel.

In the forward position, the manager can see for himself the difficulty of fulfilling his own directives. It's one thing to sit behind the desk and mandate that the sales force never discount below a certain threshold or that the assembly line increase production by ten percent; it's quite another to experience the challenges and obstacles for oneself. The manager in the forward position has real-time information, unfiltered by subordinates. He also has on-the-spot decision-making powers; in a sales situation, he can close the deal in the customer's office without going back and forth through intermediaries. And, a manager who has spent a lot of time in the "real world" is in a position to give honest assessments to his superiors, rather than just tell them what they want to hear.

Not only are the employees impressed to see managers on the front lines; the customers are impressed as well. Customers are always gratified to have a manager come by their office, even if only to get an earful of the problems encountered with the product. Letting off steam in front of somebody who is senior to the company rep they usually deal with is always more satisfying, and the higher up the person, the better. A customer will rarely say, "One of the managers of XYZ company dropped by today—what a waste of my time." Such visits make every customer feel important and also more secure, now that they have the personal backing of someone with the courage to put his own reputation on the line.

Bias Your Leaders Toward Victory

Throughout history, military leaders have allowed themselves to be driven from the field, not so much by a loss of nerve as by an inability to envision victory at that particular battle— only to find out later that the opportunity for victory had been needlessly squandered. The Marine Corps, accordingly, tries to bias its personnel to see success, rather than failure.

The very nature of the Marine Corps' specialty— amphibious warfare—demands an extremely strong focus on winning. Certainly all combat is terrifying, even under the most favorable of conditions, but what could be more disheartening than watching the ramp of your landing craft drop, revealing a totally exposed beach ahead that is being raked by machine gun fire from secure, fortified enemy positions? Yet the Marines who rushed from the protection of their landing craft onto the beaches of Iwo Jima, Okinawa, Peleliu, or Tarawa nonetheless expected to succeed.

Modern Marine Corps training continues to prepare its officers and enlisted men to see victory within their grasp, rather than defeat. As we have seen, during boot camp every recruit must overcome one challenge after another, even though at the time each obstacle or hill seems insurmountable. At no time does a drill instructor allow him to fail at one obstacle simply because he has done well on the previous ten; on the philosophy that "eight out of ten isn't bad." He must triumph over every test of will and character. A hundred times a day, recruits are reminded of the successful history of the Corps. War stories are told by their drill instructors; the weather-beaten photographs of Marine heroes are displayed against the stark landscape of the obstacle courses; the very streets the recruits walk upon (Iwo Jima Way, Chosin Blvd.) are named after the victories they study. At every turn, the message is repeated in some form or another: Victory is expected—by everyone within the Corps, by the folks back home, by the world at large, and, if the truth were to be known, by the enemy himself, many of whom suddenly find other places to be when the Marines have landed.

The very language used in training, and in Marine Corps everyday life, eschews terms that in any way suggest an attitude not totally committed to victory. For example, the army may call a combat dugout a "foxhole," but the Marines refer to it as a "fighting hole" (foxes hide in foxholes). Soldiers wear "fatigues," but Marines wear "utilities"; they are the exact same clothes, but perhaps worn with a different attitude. Marines don't "retreat," they "attack to the rear." In radio communications, the word "repeat" is forbidden (and replaced with "I say again") so that it can never be confused, in the chaos of battle, with "retreat."

The business application of the Marine Corps' way of predisposing its people to see victory rather than defeat is not simply a matter of self-hypnosis or the repetition of positive affirmations, such as "We will succeed." Marines are not brainwashed into an imperturbable confidence; they are trained to find ways to win, under the most difficult circumstances, and they taste victory often—that's why they're so confident.

There are any number of reasons why employees come to expect to lose major contracts. Many may have come from an environment of failure and look upon major triumphs as happening to other people, not themselves. Others may have an exaggerated conception of the competitor—especially if it is a very large company—and, looking at their own, very human peers, simply be unable to imagine the workforce they know triumphing over the workforce they imagine to be so dominant. Some employees, unused to the drama (and sometimes the histrionics) of negotiations, may have heard that a major customer has walked away from the conference table and, unable to recognize an "opening shot," simply decide all is lost. Employees may also be accustomed to failure because their company—before the new manager came aboard—routinely lost a lot of business.

Another, much more subtle predisposition for failure is personal jealousy. There will always be those in the organization who are not displeased to see their own company lose a big order because of their resentment of the previous successes of a peer or a rising star; they may be secretly gratified that "he wasn't able to pull it off this time." Managers who think such individuals do not exist in their departments are fooling themselves.

Whatever the reason for negative attitudes in the workplace, they can be remedied by aggressive, hearty leadership. If it's the size of the competition that seems to strike fear in the heart of his associates, the manager would do well to reflect upon the kinds of odds the 1st Marine Division faced in October 1950, during the Korean War. When no fewer than eighty thousand Communist Chinese soldiers swept across the border and encircled the ten thousand Marines at the Chosin Reservoir, Colonel Chesty Puller remarked to a frightened war correspondent, "Good—now we can attack in all directions!" It should be mentioned that the Chinese fought in an unprecedented manner, blowing bugles and attacking at night in vast overpowering waves; spreading a sense of unexpected terror throughout the UN forces along the entire Korean peninsula. At times like these, even Marines appreciate a strong leader who expects not only to survive the situation but to triumph.

One can only imagine the outcome if Colonel Puller had simply given in to the perceived supremacy of the enemy; certainly no one could have faulted him for surrendering to an 8:1 disadvantage in order to prevent the needless sacrifice of

American lives. Colonel Puller was no doubt conscious that the eye of every Marine was upon him and that whatever attitude he showed publicly would be mirrored by his command. Whether he was entirely certain of victory at the time or not, his open, cheerful defiance of the odds inspired his Marines to turn a potential rout into a stunning victory for the Marines.

The manager must remember, likewise, that the eyes of his people are upon him always and that they usually want to see the opposite of what they themselves are feeling. When his employees are anxious about completing a project on time, they want to see a manager who is confident of the outcome. When they are worried about losing a major customer, they would appreciate frank, action-oriented updates from their manager, detailing the remaining things to be done that can still influence the customer's decision. And when they are down in the mouth, a humorous, confident boss can rejuvenate the mood of the workforce. Conversely, when all are buoyant about happy rumors of an impending order, a manager with his feet planted firmly on the ground will remind everybody to keep focused until the actual contract is signed, sealed, and delivered.

When his department is up against an overwhelming competitor, he can point out the very great liabilities of being a Goliath. A huge competitor, for example, also has a huge bureaucracy, which will slow its decision-making process. The Goliath may not care as much about the pending deal (a $50,000 contract means more to a million-dollar company than it does to a billion-dollar corporation) and, if pushed to the limit, may not fight as hard. The Goliath may also be inexperienced in the particular market of contention; lacking the core expertise, it also may lack the industrywide relationships enjoyed by the smaller competitor. And the customer may suspect that the larger contender may not be willing to do the necessary "hand holding" after the sale.

If his personnel are from an environment where failure, not achievement, has been the standard, the manager must make it clear that the company is a world unto itself—one in which winning is a fact of life. If he has a few individuals whose performance and attitude have been crippled by envy, he must show them how the well-being of every associate is inexorably tied to the success of others.

When the occasional order is lost, the manager who has built up the expectations of his personnel must now make sure they do not fall too hard. A tired and grateful boss who fought alongside his people for a big contract must put the defeat into perspective for his people. Customer relationships last many years; rarely is the loss of one contract the end of the whole story. There will be other opportunities down the line; but, in the meantime, there is much to learn by examining the perceptions of the customer that prompted him to go elsewhere. By presenting the situation in an almost biographical sense—as if he were describing a temporary setback in the otherwise illustrious career of another corporation—he will reestablish the long term view and bring back the high morale of his "troops."

"You Must Not Fail"

At the very end of The Crucible—the final three-day ordeal of boot camp—exhausted recruits stagger into a small theater. They have just received their globe and anchor on the top of Grim Reaper. Although the public graduation ceremony is a week away, they are now officially Marines. On several large-screen monitors, the image of their commandant appears. The commandant, like every other Marine Corps general the authors have ever seen, is as fit as a fiddle. He looks as if he could personally lead a company of Marines on a ten-mile run. Hands on his hips, facing the camera straight on, the commandant gives an inspiring graduation "speech" (although it seems unrehearsed) to an audience that has just now been accepted into the family of Marines. He reminds the exhausted, proud new Marines in the room that they have been transformed by their basic training and that the change will last forever. He describes his experiences as a young Marine, citing an act of heroism he personally witnessed that crystallized for him the true meaning of the Corps: Marines fight for each other. At the end of this brief but goosebump-raising talk, the camera moves closer to the commandant's face. He reminds each Marine of his awesome responsibility to the nation, ending with the words "You must not fail."

It is amazing how many Marines—from boot camp graduates to veterans—take these words seriously.

For many in today's soothing culture of forgiveness, the admonition "You must not fail" seems cruelly insensitive and anachronistic, dating back to harsher times, when there were clear distinctions between success and failure. In modern society, failure is not only accepted, it is regularly expected and dealt with by our institutions with understanding and compassion. Many of the very recruits the commandant has addressed have come from families and cultures where failure is a way of life, from one generation to another.

Yet the commandant does not mince words. In fact, the words seem to have been carefully chosen. He could have said "You must always win," but every commander knows a battle may be lost on the road to victory. He could have said "You will not fail," but perhaps he thought that sounded too much like a self-hypnotic "positive thinking" affirmation. The words "must not" seem to admit to the very dangerous possibilities for failure on the battlefield that "must" be avoided. And the commandant is not saying, like a tyrannical boss, "You must not fail—or else!" The catastrophic consequences of a Marine Corps failure in an effort to defend the nation make one's personal fate seem irrelevant.

Could a business leader stand before his company's rank and file and issue such an unequivocal statement without appearing like a caricature out of Dickens? He can, if he delivers his words with as much conviction and sincerity as the commandant. It's one thing to talk down to the workforce from "on high," like a stern patriarch; it's quite another to stand in the trenches, eye to eye with the "troops," and communicate to them the absolute necessity of not failing at their task. And that is exactly the impression given by the commandant in his speech to the graduate Marines. The camera is close—one somehow has the impression that danger is near. The words "You must not fail" are not shouted, they are spoken with the conviction of someone who feels the same awesome responsibility and the same unwillingness to let down those who did not fail before him. Listening, the young Marines in the room and their veteran instructors nod their heads in silent acknowledgment.

In terms of the company's survival, the injunction "not to fail" is just as critical as it is in the defense of the nation; it's just that CEOs are generally shy about using the imperative. They would much rather speak of "working together toward a common goal," using positive words to inspire and avoiding the negative. But, why not verbalize what is implicit in the employment contract? The company, no matter how big and powerful, is in a fight for its life; if its associates fail at their respective tasks, it will be vanquished. Every manager, staff member, and employee should feel the same awesome sense of responsibility for the fate of the company as those Marines feel for the fate of the nation after the commandant's address.

The reluctance of many CEOs to appear "hokey" or old-fashioned before their more youthful workforce truly limits their ability to inspire. Forgetting that their employees are looking for a *leader*, many CEOs want to be accepted as a peer who just happens to have silver hair and the charge of the company. In pep talks, they try to speak the language of the audience. But "You must not fail" is not part of the lexicon of the modern workplace; the corporate leader has to make it so—just as the commandant has had to replace the attitude of many recruits who come from environments where failure is a way of life. And to do so, the CEO must never be afraid to expose himself to the imitations of the company clowns and cynics. There will always be those he cannot reach, but the vast majority of the workplace will respond to his mandate—as long as it is delivered with the sincerity of one who realizes that he, also, "must not fail."

This message should be reinforced as often as possible. It should become a kind of company motto, seen on all internal communications. Upper management might even consider creative wall posters to convey the message. Instead of the generic motivational scenes we see on the walls of businesses today (people paddling together in whitewater rapids or diving for a football in flight), company-specific placards could exhort each and every associate not to fail at his tasks. Many business leaders today do not remember the incredible psychological impact of America's propaganda posters of World War II. "Corny" by today's standards, these posters reached the hearts and minds of citizens and soldiers alike, convincing them of the seriousness of the situation and of the importance of their personal efforts.

Imagine an organization in which the majority of its creative and intelligent individuals walked around all day with the thought "I must not fail" in the back of their minds. Such an organization would be formidable indeed.

Leadership Strategies Checklist

—Create a "culture of courage."
—Understand that the business skills of the past have not been rendered obsolete by technology.
—Make your employees feel as if they are doing the most important jobs in the world.
—Assign realistic and attainable goals.
—Make every employee believe he or she is on the "front lines."
—Never be lulled into a "peacetime" mentality.
—Know your competition (and prevent it from knowing you).
—Don't push your personnel; inspire them to follow you.
—Prepare your people to see victory within their grasp, rather than defeat.
—"You must not fail."

Some Former Marines Who Became Successful Business Leaders

Vernon R. Loucks Jr.	Chairman/CEO	Baxter International
William S. Cashel Jr.	Former Chairman	Campbell Soup Company
Michael P. Capriano	Senior Partner	Capriano, Lichtman & Flach
Arthur Lichtman	Partner	Capriano, Lichtman & Flach
Dan Rather	Network Anchor	CBS Evening News
Nicholas Corea	Creative Consultant	CBS Productions
George Roeder	Vice Chairman	Chase Manhattan Bank
Robert Lutz	President	Chrysler Corporation
Thomas Monaghan	Chairman	Domino's Pizza
Bill Donaldson	Managing Partner	Donaldson, Lufkin and Jenrette
Thomas Faught	President	Dravo Corporation
Charles G. Guliedge	Vice Chairman/CEO & Director	Dynalect
John T. Fey	Chairman	Equitable Life Assurance Society
Ed Miller	President	Equitable Life Assurance Society
Lawrence G. Rawl	Former CEO	Exxon Corporation
Fredrick W. Smith	Chairman/CEO	Federal Express Corporation
Charles Swope	Chairman/President	First National Bank
John E. O'Toole	President	Foote, Cone & Belding Technology Group
Donald Peterson	Former Chairman	Ford Motor Company
Edward P. Lenahan	Publisher	Fortune Magazine

Leo Williams	Executive VP	General Motors Corporation
Dick Jackson	CEO	Georgia Federal Bank
Theodore Black	CEO	Ingersol-Rand
Ron Meyer	COO	MCA-Universal Studios, Inc.
Walt Burzinski	Asst VP of Finance & Administration	Merrill Lynch
Lewis T. Preston	Former Chairman	Morgan Guaranty Trust
Doug Hamlin	VP/Publisher	Motor Trend
Alexander S. Throwbridge	President	National Association of Manufacturers
Hugh McColl Jr.	CEO	NationsBank
Jimmy Glenn	President/CEO	New Mexico Retailers Association
John J. Phelan	Former Chairman/CEO	New York Stock Exchange
Walter Mattson	President	New York Times
Arthur Ochs Sulzberger	Chairman Emeritus	New York Times
Robert Levin	Senior Vice President—Planning & Development	NYMEX
A. Robert Abboud	Former President	Occidental Petroleum
John Elliott Jr.	Chairman Emeritus	Ogilvy & Mather Int'l
Harold L. Oppenheimer	Chairman	Oppenheimer Industries
Walter Anderson	Editor	Parade Magazine
Richard J. Durrel	Publisher	People Magazine
George V. Grune	CEO	Reader's Digest Association
Robert E. Coleman	Chairman/CEO	Riegel Textiles Company
Jeff Dorroh	Manager of Terminal Services	Ronald Reagan National Airport
George Gund III	Owner	San Jose Sharks
Vincent E. Sardi Jr.	Owner	Sardi's Restaurants
Joseph B. Flavin	Chairman	Singer Corporation
John A. Meyers	Vice President	Time Inc.
Richard J. Monroe	Former President/CEO	Time, Inc.
Richard Essau	VP Human Resources	The Turner Corporation
Louis F. Bantle	Chairman	U.S. Tobacco
Millie Wilkerson	VP/Area Sales Manager	Wachovia Bank
Tony Palminteri	Vice President	Western Bank

Index